The "Perfectionist's" How To Book II

Drapery
"Top Treatments"

By
Dolores "Dee" P. Lederer

Published By
Lederer Enterprises
P.O. Box 5856
Asheville, N.C. 28813

Printed in USA

WINDOWS

As eyes are the personality of a soul, windows are the personality of a home. Windows without treatments *(draperies, shades, shutters etc.)* are like eyes without eyelashes, or fine paintings without frames.

INDEX

SECTION 1

DRAPERY TOP TREATMENTS

Top treatments are used to enhance both formal and informal settings, giving a finished look to draperies *(and other window coverings)* whether they are opened or closed.

Many architectural flaws *(such as windows of different heights and styles)* can be hidden with top treatments, since they usually cover the space from the ceiling to the top of the glass.

There are two basic types of top treatments: Valance made of fabric; Cornices made of wood.

The numerous valance styles, in this book, encompass: Swags *(Empire, Austrian, Queen Anne and my own design)*; Lambrequins *(many variations with and without jabots and trim, as well as quilted and woven)*; Shirred; Pleated *(French, double, cartridge, reverse and box)*.

Cornice styles are nearly as versatile as valances. They can be: Upholstered, to match or coordinate with draperies and furnishings; Painted or stained to match furniture, walls or woodwork.

All swags *(and most other treatments)* should be mounted at the ceiling *(beamed, molded or extra high ceilings excepted)* with the high point, of the swag or cut out, even with or slightly below the top of the glass. Straight bottoms should be approximately (2"- 3") over the glass.

Suggestions given here are for standard (8'-9') ceilings. *(The windows are usually set higher for 9' ceilings.)*

The **MAXIMUM** depth of the top treatment is determined by the height of the ceiling and where it is used. For example: The depth at the low point of a ceiling mounted swag or any other treatment, should be about ($1/5$) of the total, ceiling to floor measurement; The low point of the top treatment, mounted just above the window, over long draperies should never be more than ($1/6$) nor less than ($1/7$) of the total length.

The **MINIMUM** depth: The low point of cornices and lambrequins over short draperies is (9") and (7") over shades and blinds; Pleated valances is (11") over short draperies, shades or blinds and (12") over long draperies.

Following these suggestions will keep the line and balance of the top treatments in good perspective of the design.

SECTION 2

TERMINOLOGY FOR TOP TREATMENTS

AUSTRIAN SWAG: Is a valance made with shirring between the scallops.

BIAS CUT: Is the (45°) diagonal direction of the fabric.

BOX PLEATED: Is a tailored style valance with the pleats folded flat against the board.

BRACKETS: Are the angle brackets used to support the valance boards and cornices. *(Also called corner irons.)*

BUTTERFLY PLEATS: Are single pleats or two or three pleats close together, with a wide (10"- 12") space between them.

CARTRIDGE PLEATS: Are pleats that are stuffed into round cartridges rather than folded and bar-tacked.

CASCADES: Are the finishing side pieces, cascading from the swags to a point about ($\frac{1}{3}$ - $\frac{1}{2}$) the length of the draperies. *(Sometimes used the full length of the draperies.)*

CEILING CLIPS: Are small clips that hold a rod against the ceiling.

CEILING MOUNT: Is the term used for mounting valances and cornices against the ceiling.

CORNICE: Is a box made of wood and upholstered with fabric *(stained or painted).*

CORDING: Is the welt or covered cord used on upholstered cornices *(bedspreads, pillows etc.)*

CUT OUT: Is the designed *(cut out)* edge of a valance or cornice.

DROP: Is the term used to designate the lowest point of a swag or other top treatment.

FINISHED SEAM: Is made by serging the raw edges to keep them from fraying *(or sewing a zig-zag stitch near the edge, then trimming it and sewing a straight stitch ($\frac{3}{8}$") from the edge).*

GIMP: Is the braidlike trim used on some top treatments and to finish the inside of cornices.

HIGH POINT:	Is the highest point of a swag, scallop or other cut out, at the bottom of a valance or cornice.
INSIDE MOUNT:	Is the term used for mounting cornices or valances *(shades, blinds, shutters)* inside a recessed area *(bay, bow or window frame)*.
INSTALL:	Is to mount the valances, brackets and rods on the boards or cornices and to mount the valances boards and cornices on the wall.
JABOTS:	Are decorative *(usually tie shaped)* pieces, placed to cover the seams, between the scallops or swags of a valance.
KICK PLEAT:	Is an inverted pleat on a valance *(or bedskirt)* used to conceal a seam or give fullness to a corner.
KNIFE EDGE:	Is made by pressing a seam *(so a fold is pressed near the stitching on both the face and facing side)* on the edge of a swag or cascade.
LAMBREQUIN:	Is a straight hanging valance, usually with a cut out edge.
LOW POINT:	Is the deepest *(lowest)* point of a swag or cut out of a valance or cornice.
MOUNT:	Is used interchangeably with install.
OPENING:	Is the front of a recessed area *(bay, bow, dormer)* or the inside measurement of a window.
PLEATED:	Is the term used for the common, French *(pinch)* pleats of most draperies.
QUEEN ANNE SWAG:	The most well known of all swag styles.
REVERSE PLEAT:	Is a pleat made with the folds reversed from the French pleat with the center of it covering the folds.
SERGE:	Is the term used for sewing with an overlock *(serging)* machine, to make a finished seam.
SWAG:	Is a valance *(or drapery)* folded into soft graceful folds.

It is also the name given to an individual piece in a valance.

TAKE UP: Is the amount of fabric that is taken up in the folds of the hems, pleats or eased onto the heading. Also, the amount taken up when using rod pockets.

VALANCE: Is the term used for top treatment made of fabric.

SECTION 3

THE SHIRRED VALANCE

Shirred valances are made in the same manner as shirred draperies *(See Book 1 Section 18)*. The shirring can be done with rod pockets, shirring tape or just cords.

There are many types of rods to choose from and they come in various sizes from (⅜″) to (4½″). Large wood poles (1⅜″) and (2″) are very popular and can be used with finials or elbows.

If exact lengths are critical, check the take up of the rod and allow for the extra length needed, before cutting the fabric.

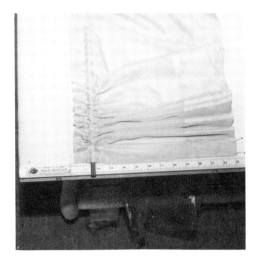
Small rod take up

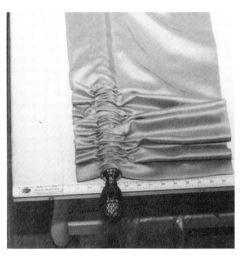
Large rod take up

When long rods are used, make button holes in the back of the rod pockets to accommodate the support brackets. Indicate the spacing of the brackets on the work sheet for reference when installing.

Make buttonhole

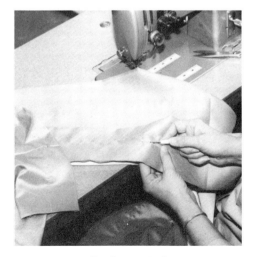
Cut buttonhole

5

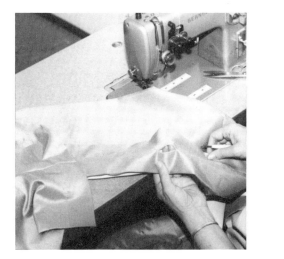

Opened buttonhole

Support bracket in place

When using a rod with finials, press and pin the top hem in place. Unfold the hem near the sides and sew a (¾"- 1") tuck, parallel to the side hem, the distance of the return (3½", 6", 8") ending about an inch below the finished hem.

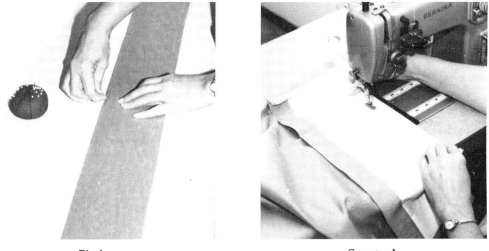

Pin hem   Sew tuck

Slit the fold to about (½") above the hem line and clip it at an angle half way to the stitching. Finish the seam with a zig-zag stitch, press the seam open and sew the hem and rod pocket. Open the seam on the right side of the rod pocket to insert the rod.

Slit fold above hem line

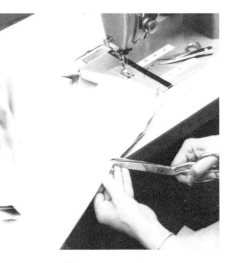

Clip at an angle

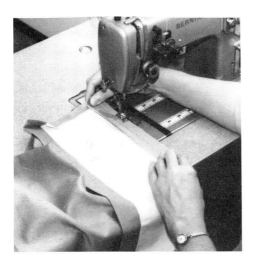

Finish seam edges

Sew header ruffle

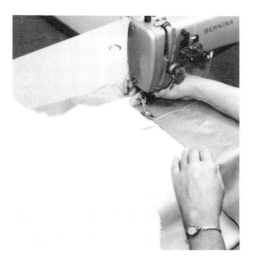

Sew rod pocket

Open seam in rod pocket

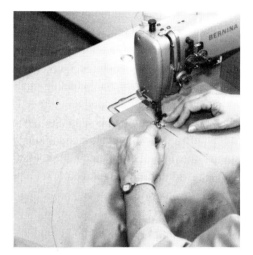

Bar-tack top and bottom

Make tuck

Finished side

Inserted rod

Rods can be supported from the ceiling with drop ceiling clips, to accommodate a header ruffle. *(Know your hardware.)*

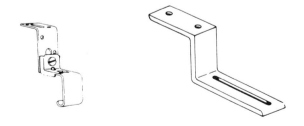

Ceiling clips

SECTION 4

THE FRENCH PLEATED VALANCE

The French pleated valance is probably the most extensively used of all top treatments. It is a natural for "Early American" or any other country style decor, and can be quite dressy when trim is used. A pleated valance should be at least (11") deep *(4" heading and 7" skirt)* but, can be made any appropriate length to cover the area between the ceiling and (2") or so over the glass.

The instructions for making a pleated valance are the same as for pleated draperies. *(See Book I Sections 6 - 16.)*

The spaces in CUSTOM draperies and valances should be (3½"- 4") except for sheer fabrics which should be pleated with approximately (3") spaces. The pleats should take up (5½"- 6") and never less than (5") in standard French or reverse pleats. *(See Section 5 for other style pleats.)*

A simple way to customize *(make sure all of the seams are hidden from view, all pleats are the same sizes and all spaces are the same size)* is to plan (5) pleats and (5) spaces in each panel *(width)* of (48") fabric or (6) pleats and (6) spaces in 54") fabric. Trim the outside panels to include the hems and returns and the number of pleats and spaces needed for the finished width of the valance. *(See Book I Section 10.)*

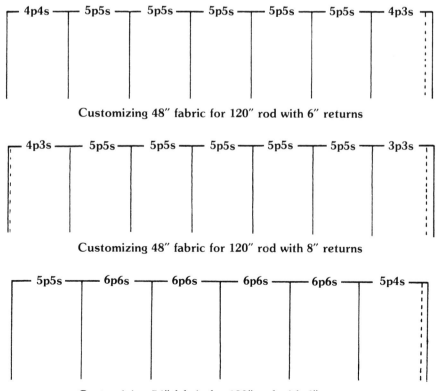

Customizing 48" fabric for 120" rod with 6" returns

Customizing 48" fabric for 120" rod with 8" returns

Customizing 54" fabric for 120" rod with 6" returns

9

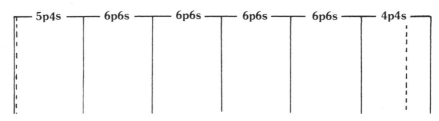

| 5p4s | 6p6s | 6p6s | 6p6s | 6p6s | 4p4s |

Customizing 54″ fabric for 120″ rod with 8″ returns

A few pieces of tape on the sewing machine enables you to sew accurately and increase your speed.

The following items will be needed to set up the machine: Vinyl tape measures or ruler tape *(comes in a roll and measures up to 10″ and then repeats)*; Double face scotch tape; (½″) vinyl scotch tape; and clear finger nail polish or varathane.

Using the double face tape, place the tapes on the machine, measuring out from the needle hole, as in the pictures.

Trim the tape measures from the needle and the throat plate, even with the (½″) tape on the RH side. Leave enough of the tape measure on the LH side to tuck in. Coat over the tapes with varathane or clear nail polish, so they will not wear off.

Attach a tape measure along the front of the sewing machine table, for measuring the total distance of the spaces or pleats in each panel.

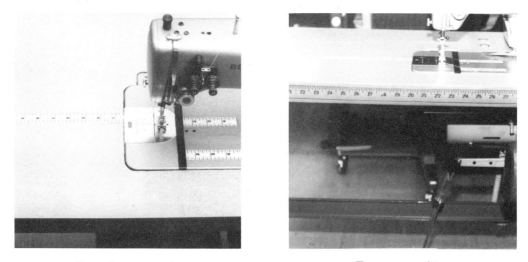

Tapes for measuring   Tape on machine

The tape on the LH side lets you measure the overlaps, returns and spaces between the pleats at a glance. The top tape on the RH side is used to measure the pleats and the bottom tape is to help keep the pleat square. *(There is no need to premark the pleats.)*

10

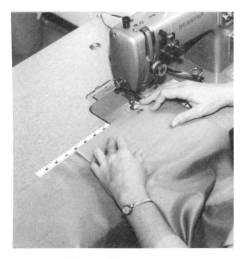

Measuring spaces

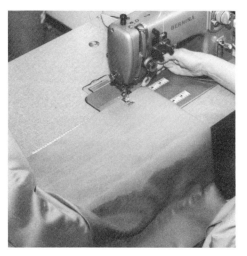

Measuring pleats

The (½″) tape is used as a guide for sewing the lining in. Place it (⅞″) from the needle hole, perfectly straight from the edge in the front. The RH side of the tape is used to measure the side seams, and the LH side is used for the top seam. This makes the (⅛″) allowance that is needed in the folds of the hems and heading. (*See Book I Section 16.*)

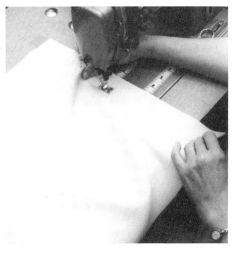

Measure the side seam

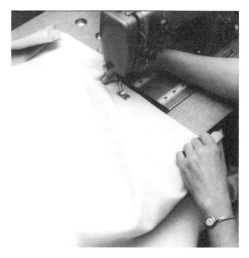

Measure the top seam

SECTION 5

THE BUTTERFLY PLEATED VALANCE

The Butterfly style is a more formal valance and is usually hung from a ceiling mounted rod. It is a combination of pleats and large scalloped spaces between them.

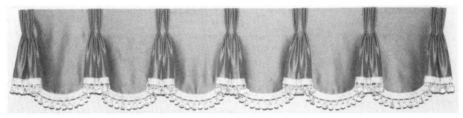

Butterfly pleated valance with French pleats

This style of valance should be at least (12″) deep at the high point with the scallops about (2″- 2½″) deep. It should come down over the window far enough to conceal the frame.

French pleats are the most popular, using two regular pleats (1″- 1¼″) apart or a single double folded one. The cartridge style pleat is more attractive if two or three pleats (1¼″- 1½″) apart, are used between the large (10″- 12″) scalloped spaces.

French or reverse pleats should be (5½″- 6″), allow (7″- 8″) for double French pleats and (3″- 4½″) for cartridge pleats.

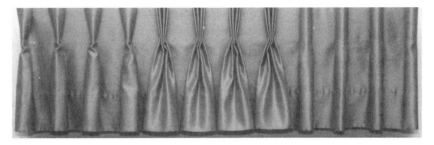

Reverse pleats   Double French pleats   Cartridge pleats

To calculate the number of panels (widths) needed, determine the style of the pleats and the number and size of the pleats and spaces that will fit the length of the rod being used. The panels will be trimmed to the width needed plus the seam allowances. When using patterns, plan each large space and set of pleats to show the same part of the pattern. This can take (1 or 2) more panels and the pattern will **not** match, at the seams, when they are trimmed to size, but they will be completely behind the pleated fold and will not show or detract.

Example: 1. 120″ rod: 8″ returns, 3″ hems, 2 French pleats 5½″, 48″ fabric, 10 large spaces, 11 small spaces, ⅜″ seam allowances.

$120″ - 11s × 1″ = 109″ ÷ 10s = 10.9″s$
$3″h + 8″r, + 2p × 5½″, + 1s × 1″, + 1s × 10.9″ = 33.9 + sa = 1w$
$4p × 5½″, + 2s × 10.9″, + 2s × 1, = 45.8 + sa = 1w × 4, = 4w$
$4p × 5½″, + 2s × 1″, + 1s × 10.9″, + 8″r + 3″h = 45.9″ + sa = 1w$
$1w + 4w + 1w = 6w.$

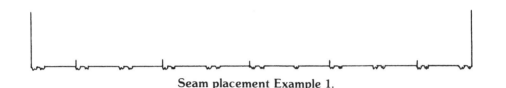

Seam placement Example 1.

Example: 2. 120″ rod: 8″ returns, 3″ hems, 4¼″ cartridge pleats, 48″ fabric, 9 large spaces, 20 small spaces, ⅜″ seam allowances.

$120″ - 20s × 1¼″ = 95″ ÷ 9 = 10.56″s$
$3″h + 8″r, + 2s × 1¼″, + 3p × 4¼″, + 1s × 10.56″ = 37.56″ + sa = 1w$
$6p × 4¼″, + 4s × 1¼″, + 1s × 10.56″ = 42.56″ + sa × 3 = 3w$
$2s × 10.56″, + 3p × 4¼″, + 2s × 1¼″ = 36.41″ + sa × 2 = 2w$
$1s × 10.56″, + 3p × 4¼″, + 8″r + 3″h = 34.31″ + sa = 1w$
$1w + 3w + 2w + 1w = 7w.$

Seam placement Example 2.

The cut length of the fabrics is (2½″) longer than the finished length. *(RAILROAD the lining whenever possible to eliminate the seams).* If seamed lining is used, trim the panels to the same widths as the face fabric panels, so the seams can be placed together to avoid having unsightly shadows of the seams showing. *(Self line a scalloped valance if trim is not used.)*

Cut the number of panels needed and trim them to the proper width. Sew the panels together from the bottom to the top and press the seams to the left.

Lay the seamed fabric right side up, with the bottom edge against the table ruler. Then, lay the lining on it wrong side up with the bottom edge (⅛″) from the ruler. If the lining is seamed, align the seams with the seams in the face fabric, square the top so the valance is (1½″) longer than the finished length and pin the edges together.

13

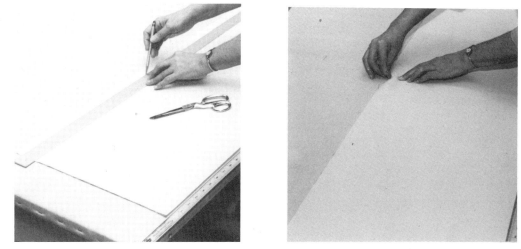

Square top edges

Pin edges together

Move the lining down even at the bottom and pin the seams together. Mark the stitching line of the scallops (½″) from the bottom edge and pin it in place.

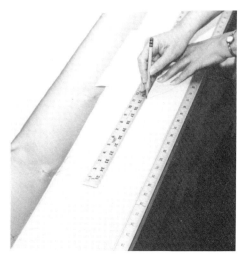

Mark stitching line

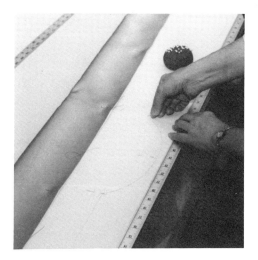

Pin bottom

Sew the bottom seam, trim it to about (¼″) and clip the corners. Then with the lining side up, sew across the top using a (⅞″) seam. Turn the face side up and sew the heading to the seam allowance so it is even with the stitching.

Sew along pattern line

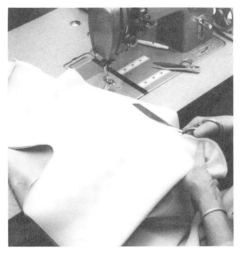

Trim seam

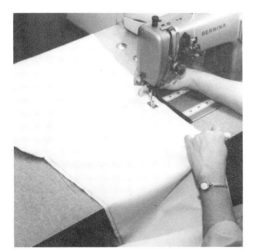

Sew top seam

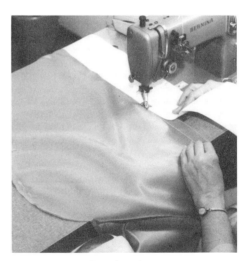

Sew heading

Turn the valance right side out and press the bottom into a knife edge. Then, press the heading so the face fabric shows about (¹⁄₁₆″) on the lining side.

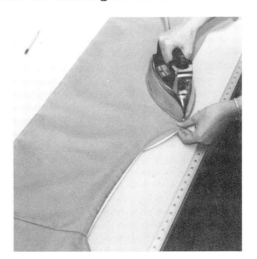

Press knife edge

Press heading

15

Trim the lining (3") narrower on the sides and press (1½") double hems. Blind stitch them in place and sew the corners by hand.

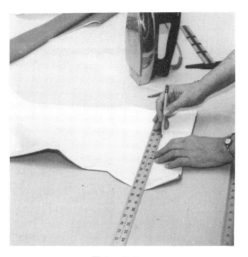

Trim lining

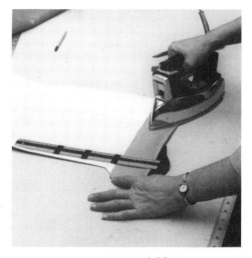

Press first fold

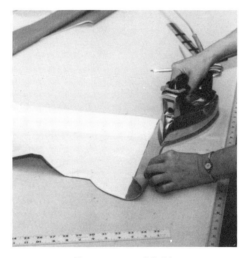

Press second fold

If you do not have a walking foot machine, glue the fringe in place before sewing it. *(This helps to keep it from puckering.)*

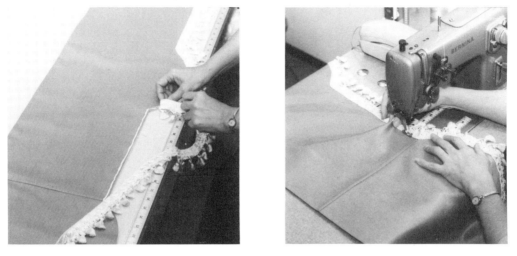

Glue fringe   Sew fringe

Measure a panel and determine the exact size the pleats will be. They will be a little smaller than planned, due to the **take up** *(See Section 2)*. Accuracy is a must since the valance has to fit **tight** on the rod.

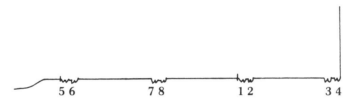

5 6   7 8   1 2   3 4

Pleating sequence for Example 1.

Starting at the RH side, sew the pleat by the seam, first. *(This keeps the fabric square on the heading.)* Then measure the small space and sew the next pleat. Check the width of the large space and sew another pleat. Fold the return back, measure the small space and sew the corner pleat. Continue pleating across the valance in this manner, then, bar-tack the pleats *(See Book I Section 16).*

Sew pleat by seam   Measure small space

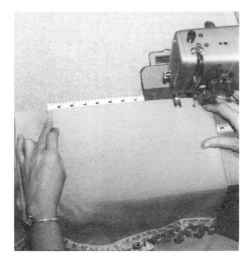

Measure large space

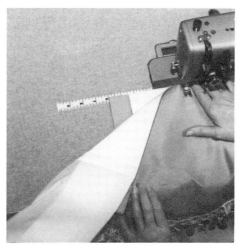

Measure return

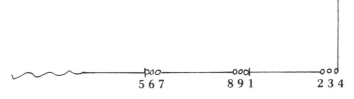

5 6 7   8 9 1   2 3 4

Pleating sequence for Example 2.

To make a reverse pleat, hold the outside of the pleat between the fingers of one hand and slightly flatten the front of it with the other hand. Close the pleat over the center folds and adjust it, so the sides are close to the stitching. Sew the bar-tack about (½″) from the bottom and (¼″) from the back of the pleat.

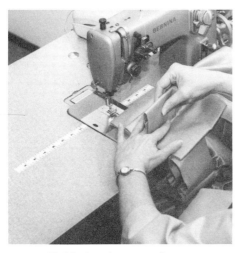

Hold pleat between fingers

Flatten center

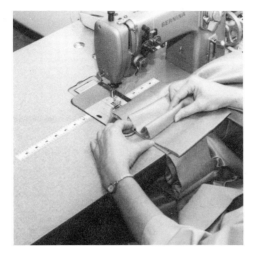

Close over folds

Crease folds

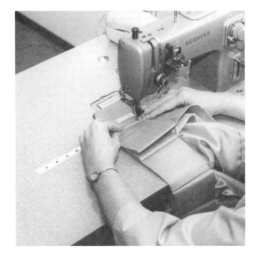

Bar-tack pleat

Finished pleat

To make a double French pleat, insert your forefinger in the pleat to spread it open. Center the fold on the seam and crease the two folds, then, flatten each fold onto the seam and close the pleat. Bar-tack about (½″) from the bottom and about half way between the front and back of the pleat.

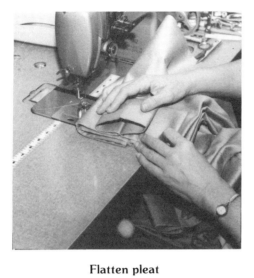

Flatten pleat

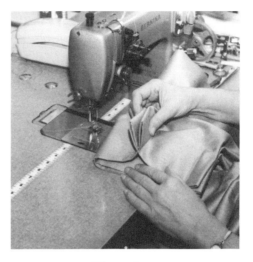

Close pleat

Flatten half pleat

Crease folds

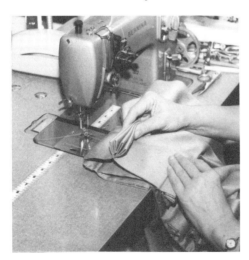

Close pleat

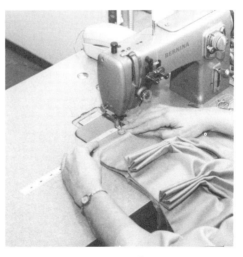

Bar-tack pleat

The cartridge pleats can be shaped by stuffing them with rolled up strips of bonded polyester batting or tissue paper.

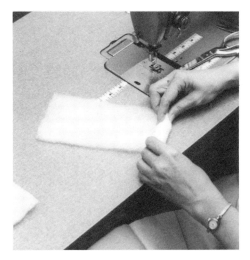

Roll the core

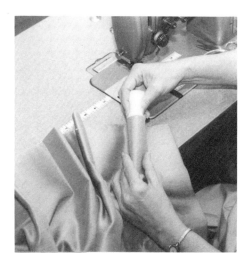

Insert core

Cartridge pleats

SECTION 6

THE BOX PLEATED VALANCE

The box pleated style has a tailored look and is very attractive with traditional furnishings or it will soften an otherwise stark contemporary setting.

The pleats are made in triple folds. Usually all of the pleats are the same size ranging from (4"- 12"). However, combinations of large and small pleats are attractive.

Box pleated valances can be from (7") deep, when used with shades or blinds *(on inside mounts)* up to any appropriate length to cover the area above the window, from the ceiling to about (2") or so over the glass.

To calculate the number of panels *(widths)* needed for seamed or printed fabric, determine the number and size of pleats that will fit on the valance board being used. Multiply the size of the pleat by (3) and divide that number into the width of the fabric. Then, add another panel *(sometimes more)* for the corner pleats, returns and hems. This customizes *(places the seam and pattern in the same position on each pleat)* the valance at the same time. The seams and patterns will fall in the same place in each panel. *(Add seam allowances.)*

Example:

1. 60" board = 5, 12" pleats: 12" × 3 = 36" per pleat; 48" ÷ 36" = 1 pleat per panel.
   1 × 5 = 5 panels + 1 panel = 6 panels.

2. 60" board = 12, 5" pleats: 5" × 3 = 15" per pleat; 48" ÷ 15" = 3 pleats per panel.
   12 ÷ 3 = 4 panels + 1 panel = 5 panels.

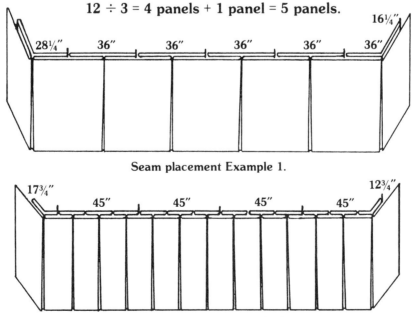

Seam placement Example 1.

Seam placement Example 2.

22

The cut width when RAILROADING the fabric *(and lining)* will be (3) times the length of the valance board, plus the corner pleats, returns and hems.

Example: **1.**   12″ pleats, 60″ board: = 60″ × 3 = 180″ + 24″ corner pleats + 14½″ returns + 6″ hems = 224½″.

              2.   5″ pleats, 60″ board: = 60 × 3 = 180″ + 10″ corner pleats + 14½″ returns + 6″ hems = 204½″.

When using plain fabric, the cut length is the finished length plus (11″). The cut length for lining is the finished length plus (7½″). Patterned fabrics *(printed or woven)* will be cut at the completion of the pattern repeat beyond the proposed cut length. If the valance is less than (11″) deep, make a smaller hem.

Cut the lining and the number of panels needed. Add the seam allowances to the designated width and trim the panels to the proper size and seam them together.

Press a double (4″) hem in the face fabric and a double (2¾″) hem in the lining. Blind stitch the hems in place.

Cut the lining (6″) narrower than the face fabric. Then, with the right sides together and the lining (1″) from the bottom, pin and sew the side seams (1⅜″). Turn the valance right side out and press a (1½″) hem around the side seams. Blind stitch the corners by hand in the same manner as draperies *(See Book I Section 11).*

Sew side seams

Press hem around seam

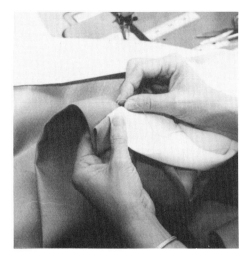

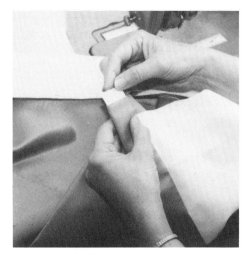

Hand stitch corner   Insert weight

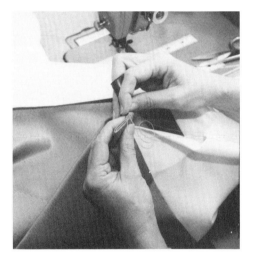

Close bottom

    To table the valance, place it lining side up, with the hem against the table ruler. Mark the cutting line, allowing (2″) for stapling it on the board and pin the top edges together.

Square top edges

Serge or make a finished seam across the top. *(This keeps it from fraying when it is cleaned.)* Mark the returns and folds, then, pin the pleats in place.

Make finished seam

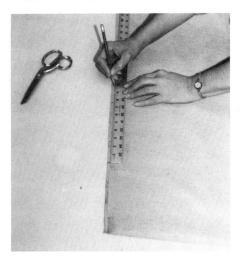

Mark folds

Pin folds

Press lightly

Prepare the board *(See Section 15)* and draw a line (2″) from the front edge. Mark the placement of each pleat and staple the valance in place. If the fabric is light weight, it could be attached with velcro *(See Section 7)*.

Mark board

Staple valance in place

Turn it upside down and mount the brackets and rods *(See Section 15)*.

Many variations of the box pleated valance can be made. Customize each panel according to the number and size of the pleats being used. Alternate a small pleat and a large one or use two or three small ones between the large ones.

For an interesting variation, scallop the bottom of the valance or using a combination of sizes, scallop the large ones and leave the small ones straight.

Still another variation, use small box pleats between large single spaces. *(Customize each panel in the same manner.)*

A decorative or contrasting border on a straight valance is very attractive, especially if the valance is quite deep, but fringe *(tasseled or looped)* is more appropriate for scallops.

SECTION 7

THE LAMBREQUIN VALANCE

The lambrequin is a straight hanging valance, usually with a cut out or decorative edge. It is the simplest of all top treatments to make and is suitable for most fabric.

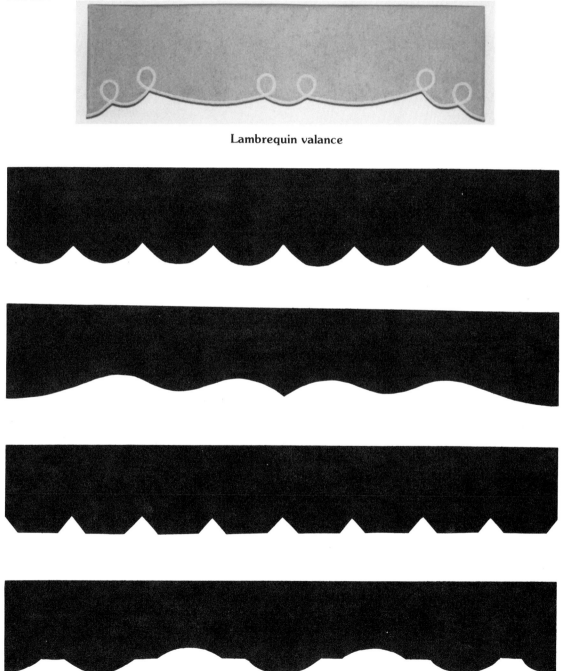

Lambrequin valance

Cut out designs

These are but a few of the hundreds of designs used on this style of valance. For additional designs *(See Section 8)* or experiment with your own ideas. Enlarge them by using graph paper.

NOTE: A printed pattern is available for Sections 8 & 9 combined.

The lambrequin is usually mounted from the ceiling, covering the frame and about (2″) of the glass *(See Section 1)*. A shorter version can be used with Roman shades *(See Book III)* either inside the frame or just above the window. It looks best if there are no seams showing, therefore, the fabric is usually RAILROADED for most designs.

Quilted lambrequins are very attractive with matching bedspreads. They can be quilted by machine or by hand. Otherwise they are made in the same manner as any other design.

Tapestry and velvet lambrequins are woven in symmetrical designs with scalloped bottom edges. They come in a variety of patterns and color combinations and are available most places where draperies are sold. *(They can be ordered unfinished.)* This is the only style that does not need to be lined.

Some variations of this style being completely straight are: Kickpleats at the corners or to conceal seams; Jabots set into seams to divide patterns or scallops.

Other variations include: Ruffles or welting sewn into the bottom seam; Bias trim enclosing the seam; Fringe *(tassle, loop or brush)* sewn on the bottom edge and/or elevated; Soutache or military braid sewn in scroll designs: Decorative borders: Buttons; Bows; Contrasting fabric showing in kickpleats or cut outs and etc. The variations cease only when the designing mind quits.

The cut width is the length of the valance board plus the returns and (1½″)

double side hems. The cut length is the finished length plus (1¾″) if the fabric is RAILROADED or (2¾″) if it has to be tabled. The lining will be the same size and should be RAILROADED to keep the seams from shadowing through. *(Add (1¼″) to the cut length when stapling it to the board.)*

Cut the fabrics to size and seam them if necessary. If decorative boarders, scroll designs or elevated trims of any kind are being used, pencil the stitching line on the face fabric. Run a bead of glue along the line and ease the trim onto it, to keep it in place as you sew. *(This also helps to keep it from puckering.)*

With the right sides of the fabrics together and the lining side up, lay them with the bottom edges against the table ruler. Mark the sewing line of the cut out design (½″) from the bottom and pin it. *(Square the top if necessary.)*

Mark sewing line

Pin in place

Trim the lining (3″) narrower than the fabric on each side, then with the lining side up sew the sides in (1⅜″) seams.

Trim lining

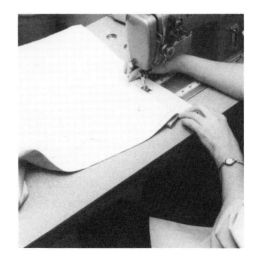

Sew seams

29

Fold the face fabric into a (1½″) pleat on each side *(this folds the hem around the seam)* then, sew across the bottom. Trim the cut out to a (¼″) seam, clip the corners and/or inside curves, turn the valance right side out and press the bottom into a knife edge.

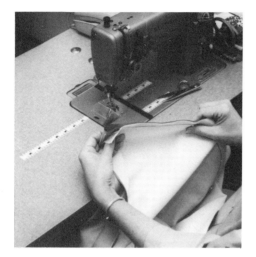

Fold LH pleat

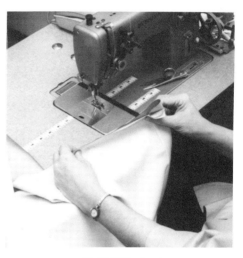

Fold RH pleat

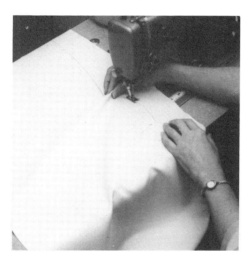

Sew on pattern line

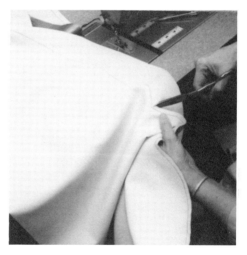

Trim seam

Press knife edge

Glue and sew the trim to the bottom edge. Insert weights into the side hem, then pin and serge the top edges together *(or make a finished seam)*.

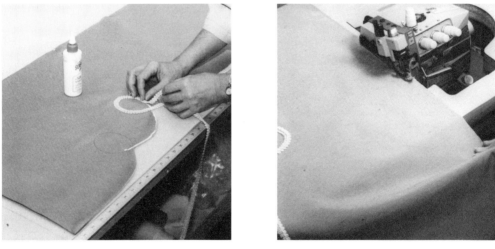

Glue trim in place   Finished seam

This is the only style that I recommend attaching to the board with velcro. Keep the valance smooth but not stretched as you sew the velcro, easing it a little at the corners. Fold the ends down and hand stitch them in place so the stitches do not show through.

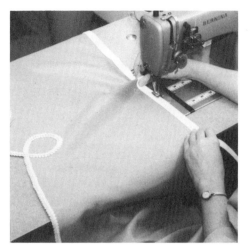
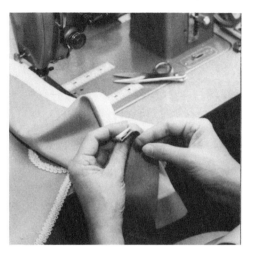

Sew velcro   Secure corners

Prepare the board *(See Section 15)* **and mark the center of both the valance and the board. Align the center marks and press the top of the valance into place.**

Align center marks   Press into place

Mount the brackets and rods on the board *(See Section 15)* **ready for installation.**

Lambrequin with set-in jabots

To make a lambrequin valance, with the jabots set into the seams, determine the size and number of scallops or pattern repeats, that will fit across the valance board less (2″). Make a pattern the size needed plus (³⁄₈″) seam allowances. Allow (1½″) double hems on the returns.

Make a pattern for the jabots *(See Section 10)* with the seam the same length as the seams of the valance. Cut one piece, then, using it as a pattern, fit it exactly on each pattern repeat. Cut the lining pieces the same size. *(Cut the jabot lining (¼″) narrower at the top.)*

Cut one piece

Match patterns

Assemble the valance with a jabot between each piece, then assemble the lining in the same manner. Press the seams toward the jabots.

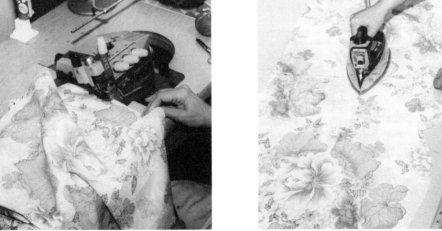

Sew from bottom   Press seams

Carefully match the seams of the lining to the seams of the valance, at the bottom and pin the edges together. Sew a (¼″) seam, clip the corners, turn it right side out and press a knife edge.

Pin seams together

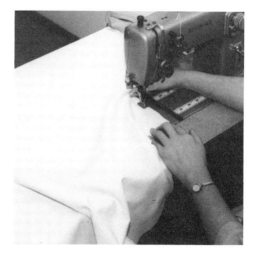
Sew bottom seam

Press knife edge

Hem the sides and attach the trim in the same manner as previously shown. Then, fold each jabot into a pleat, align the seams and pin it. Using a zipper foot, sew close to the seam from the bottom to the top.

Align seams

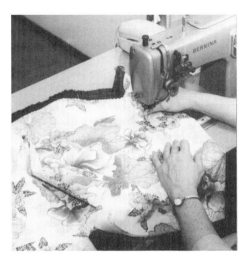

Sew close to seams

Flatten the jabots, centering them over the seams and press them lightly. Finish the top edge and attach it to the board as previously shown.

Center jabots over seams

Press lightly

SECTION 8

CORNICES

The cornice is a top treatment made of wood and is appropriate for both formal and informal settings. It has a similarity to the lambrequin.

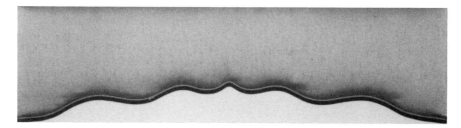

Upholstered cornice

The instructions given here are for upholstered cornices. However, there are many decorative motifs and moldings available to trim fine wood cornices, which can be stained or painted to match furniture or woodwork.

It doesn't take a master craftsman to make a cornice to be covered. Use (½″) plywood for the face and a (1″ x 6″) or (1″ x 8″) for the top. *(Redwood is light weight and warps very little.)*

These are but a few of the hundreds of designs used for cornices. For additional patterns *(See Section 7)* or experiment with your own ideas. *(Enlarge them by using graph paper.)*

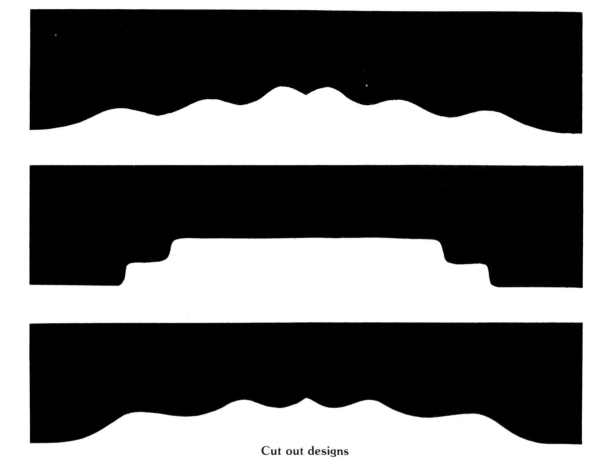

Cut out designs

NOTE: A printed pattern is available for Sections 8 & 9 combined.

Make a pattern for the design, then trace it onto the plywood and cut it out with a sabre or jig saw.

Trace pattern

Use sabre saw

Assemble the cornice, using wood glue at the seams. If the cornice has to be spliced, strap brackets can be used on the face side, since the padding will cover them. *(The ceiling board can be placed (2"- 3") from the top, if it is to be mounted against a slanted ceiling.)*

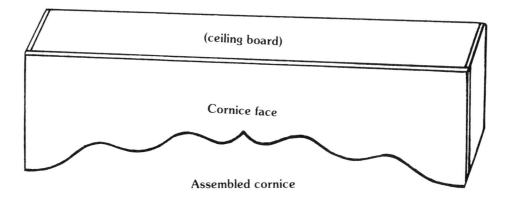

(ceiling board)

Cornice face

Assembled cornice

Cut the fabric about (6"- 7") wider than the face of the cornice plus the returns and about (3") deeper than the depth of the cornice. *(Railroad plain fabrics whenever possible to eliminate seams.)* Cut the lining (2") wider than the face of the cornice and deep enough to cover the inside *(front and ceiling)* and the outside top plus (2"). Cut the end pieces separately.

Center the pattern on the face side of the fabric and trace the pattern line. Cut it out, leaving a (½") seam allowance. Mark the lining in the same manner, but cut it on the pattern line and do not leave a seam allowance.

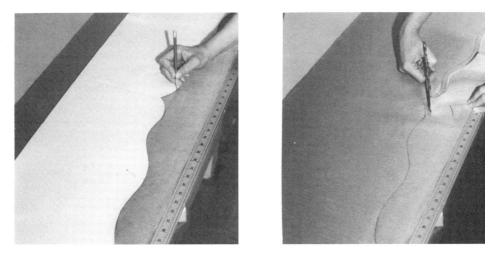

Trace pattern   Leave seam allowance

Cut enough (1¾") bias strips *(when using standard size upholstery welting)* for both the top and bottom edges of the cornice and enough (3") bias strips for the bottom edge.

38

Sew the bias strips together and press the seams open. Cover the welting with the narrow bias and sew it to the wide bias. Then, turn it over and sew it along the pattern line. *(This procedure can be done in one operation with a walking foot machine.)*

Cover welting

Sew onto wide bias

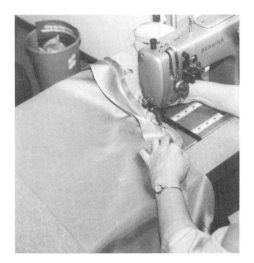

Sew onto pattern line

Spray the front and ends of the cornice, lightly, with a rubber base fabric glue and place the padding on it *(this will keep it from shifting when the fabric is stapled in place).* Trim the padding about an inch beyond the edges of the cornice, both top and bottom, then glue and smooth it in place over the edges.

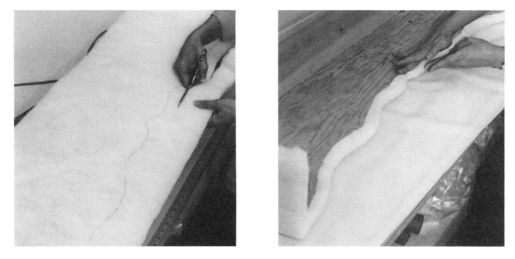

| Trim padding | Smooth edges |

With the cornice laying bottom side up, start at the center and staple through the seam allowance and tacking strip, along the bottom, with the welting fitting smoothly at the top edge.

Staple in place

Turn the cornice face side down and spray the inside near, the bottom. Smooth the wide bias strip, over the stapled edge, onto the glued area and staple it. (*This keeps it firmly and smoothly in place.*)

Spray near edges

Smooth into place

Staple in place

Set the cornice upright and spray the top near the front. Again, starting at the center, smooth the covering up over the top edge and staple it in place, near the raw edge of the fabric. Now, staple the welting along the edge and finish the corners.

Smooth covering

Staple in place

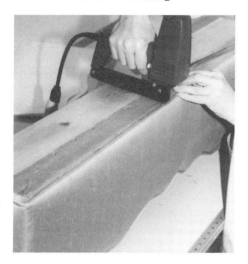

Staple welting

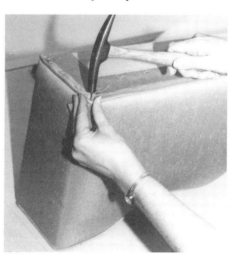

Finish corners

Spray the inside of the cornice and staple the end pieces in place, with the staples in a neat even row near the raw edge.

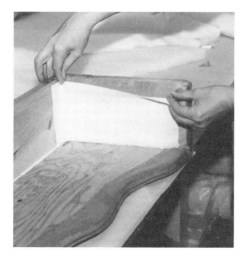

Fit end piece

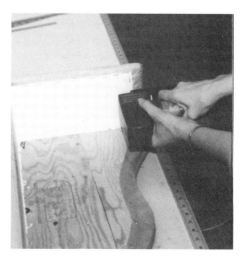

Staple near edge

42

Run a bead of glue *(such as So-Bo)* in the corners and put the lining in place with the cut out *edge* about (1″) from the bottom. Fold the ends under about (1″) and smooth the lining into place, securing it into the bead of glue with a flat tool. Then staple it in place, near the edge of the cut out.

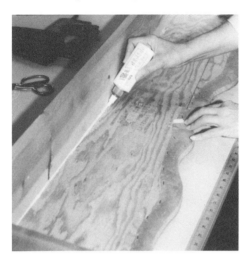

Glue corners

Fit lining in place

Secure lining in corners

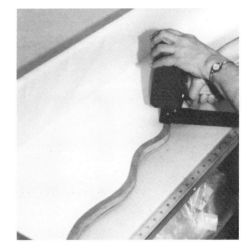

Staple near edge

Set the cornice upright and carefully spray the top. Clip the lining, at the corners and smooth it over the glued top. Turn the edge under the tacking strip and staple it in place to cover the seam allowance of the welting.

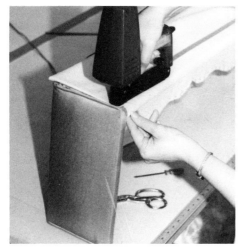

Fit corner

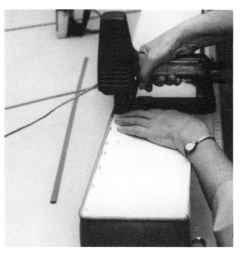

Cover raw edges

Lay the cornice face side down and run a bead of glue near the raw edge of the lining and cover the raw edge and staples with a row of gimp.

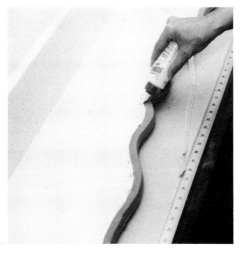

Glue raw edges

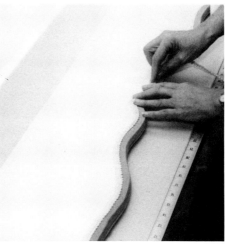

Cover with gimp

Mount the brackets and rod *(or rods)* ready for installation *(See Section 15).*

44

SECTION 9

THE EMPIRE SWAG

The Empire swag valance is a formal style of top treatment. It is very attractive, with or without trim. It can have the same effect as the Queen Anne and Original Style Swags *(Sections 12 & 14)*, but is, quite often, more versatile when working with narrow windows or corner windows of different widths.

This style is usually made on the straight of the fabric, but has a softer look when made on the bias.

Empire swag valance

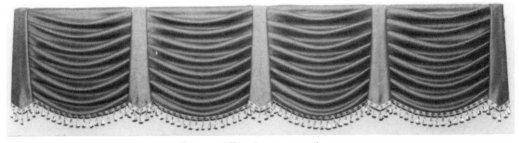

Bias cut Empire swag valance

NOTE: Printed patterns are available for Sections 9, 12 & 14 *(Sections 10 & 13 are included).*

To make a pattern, first determine the number of swags (16"- 20") that will fit across the length of the valance board being used. *(The swags will be (2") from the ends of the board.)* The depth of the swag is measured at the highest point. The center of the swag drops (3"- 3½"). Determine the number of folds by allowing (2") of coverage for each one. Add (2½") at the top (3"- 3½") inside each fold and (2¼") at the bottom to get the cut length. *(Allow (2¾") at the bottom if trim is not being used.)*

Example: 16" high point ÷ 2" folds = 8 folds.
8 × 3¼" = 26" inside folds + 16" outside folds + 2½" top +
2¼" bottom = 46¾" cut length.

45

Square a piece of paper the exact cut length and (2¾") wider than the top of a single swag *(up to (3¼") wider for bias cut swags)*. Fold the paper in half lengthwise and draw a line from the open corners on one end to a point *(up from the fold)* half the width of a single swag, plus a (⅜") seam allowance, on the other end. Then, draw a curved line from the fold at the bottom to a point (1¼") from the bottom on the side.

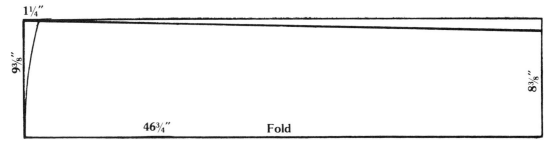

Pattern for 16" W x 16" L swag

Use the same pattern for the returns. To determine the width as (1") plus a (⅜") seam allowance on the face of the board and (3") for a double hem on the side. *(When using this pattern for an Austrian valance use (1½") single hems.)*

To calculate the yardage, figure the returns as one swag and allow (1⅜) yards for each (2) swags and (⅝) yard for (5) jabots. *(NOTE: (6) jabots will take (1¼) yards.)* Make allowances for pattern repeats when using brocades or prints.

To calculate the yardage, when using bias cut swags, allow (2) yards for the first one and (1) yard each for the others including the returns, plus the jabots *(cut on the straight grain of the fabric)*. Make allowances for pattern repeats. Cut the fabric in bias pieces, then, use the pattern.

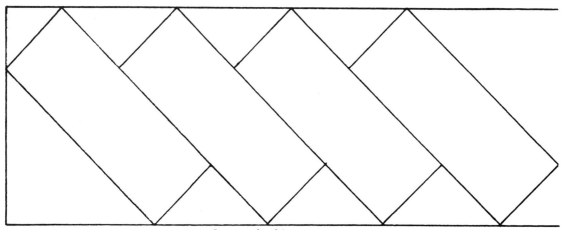

Layout for bias cut swags

Whether cutting bias or straight grained swags, cut the lining in the same manner as the swags are cut. When using patterned fabric, cut one piece using the pattern, then, use that piece as a pattern and make all of the pieces identical. Cut the jabots *(See Section 10)* on the straight of the fabric.

To assemble the valance, sew the seams from the bottom to the top. Lay a swag right side up, then, lay the LH return piece on it, wrong side up, next, lay the LH return lining right side up and finally lay a swag lining, wrong side up on top. Align the seam edges and sew the four pieces together. *(This encloses the seams.)* Continue in this manner with the swag pieces, face sides together and the lining pieces face sides together on top and finish with the RH return.

LH return in place

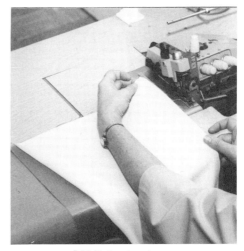

LH lining in place

Sew 4 pieces together

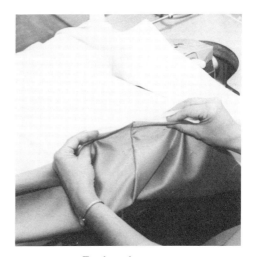

Enclosed seams

RH return in place

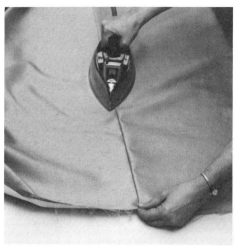

Press seams

Trim the lining (3″) narrower, on each side, than the face fabric and press a double (1½″) hem, then, blind stitch it in place. *(Press a (1½″) single hem in Austrian valances.)*

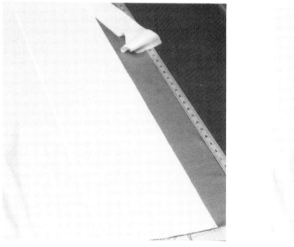

Trim lining

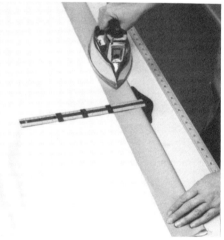

Press 1st fold

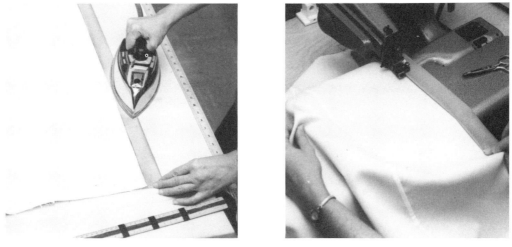

Press 2nd fold   Sew side hem

Serge, or make a finished seam, across both the top and bottom of the swag. *(This keeps it from fraying.)* With the lining side up, sew the fringe so the top edge just covers the edge of the swag and the stitching is about ($\frac{1}{4}$″) from the top of the trim. Turn the swag face side up and sew near the top edge of the trim. *(Make a small blind stitched hem if trim is not used.)*

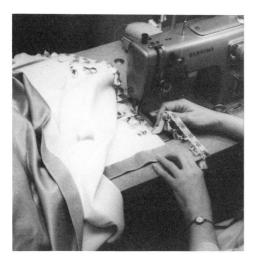

Sew on lining side

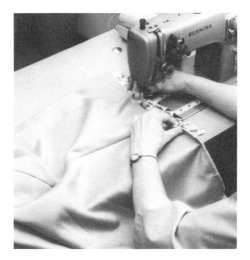

Sew on face side

Make the fold marks on the seams with the first one (2″) from the bottom and alternate with (3$\frac{3}{4}$″) and (2″) spaces. Mark the sides ($\frac{1}{2}$″) from the edge, starting from the top, even with the seam marks.

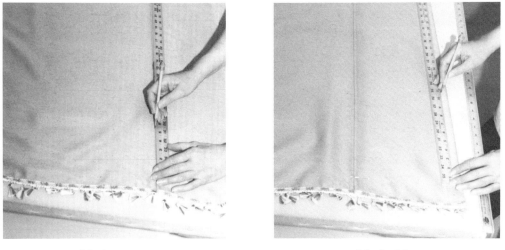

Mark seams   Mark sides

Sew the folds in place by bringing the first mark at the bottom to the second one, the third one to the fourth and etc.

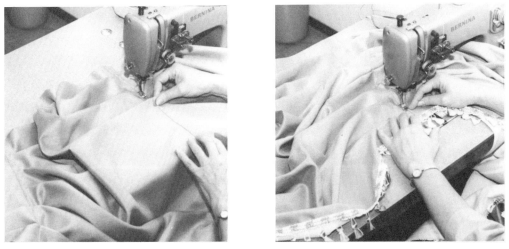

Make fold   Sew in place

Make the jabots *(See Section 10)*. Prepare the board *(See Section 15)*. Make a line on the board (2″) from the front and staple the swag in place, along the line. Center the jabots over the seams, with the high point of the jabot even with the high point of the swag and staple them in place.

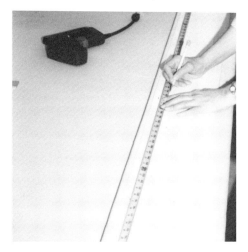

Mark swag placement

Staple in place

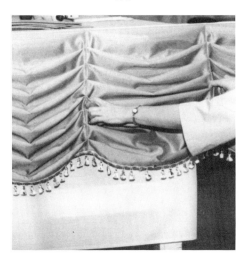

Adjust folds

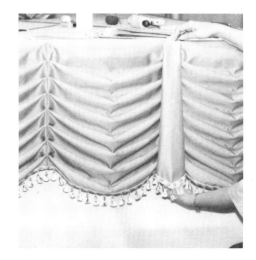

Adjust jabots

Staple jabots in place

Prepare two boards the width of the swag board (2") shorter than the swag. Attach them to the swag board with angle brackets. *(This keeps the valance from drawing in at the sides.)*

Attach end boards

Mount the brackets and rods on the board *(See Section 15)* ready for installation.

SECTION 10

JABOTS

Jabots are small decorative pieces, used to cover seams or fill spaces between swags or scallops on valances. The most common ones are simple, tie shaped pieces, with or without trim, used on the Empire and Austrian Swag Style valances.

A short double cascade makes an attractive jabot, to use with Queen Anne or my own design swags, where the tie shaped style is too narrow.

Many variations, of both the tie and the box shaped jabots, can be made to use with straight hanging lambrequins: Add a ruffle; Reverse the tie shape and use a contrast lining and/or tassel; Make a double reverse tie; Curve the bottom of a reverse tie instead of making a point; and etc.

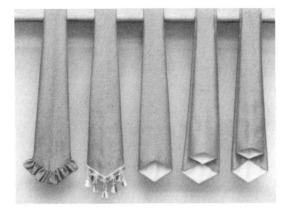

Various styles

Since box shaped jabots are cut straight and are assembled in the same manner as the tie shaped styles, instructions will be given for tie shaped only.

To make a pattern for the basic jabot, square a piece of paper (10″) wide and (5″) longer than the high point of the valance and fold it in half lengthwise. Draw a slanted line from the open corners of the LH end to a point (2¼″) from the fold on the RH end. Then, draw a line from the fold on the LH end to a point (2¾″) from the LH end on the open side. Make the pattern (¼″) narrower at the top for the lining.

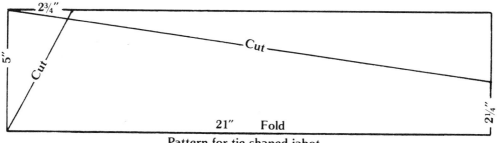

2¾"

Cut

5"

Cut

21"   Fold

2¼"

Pattern for tie shaped jabot

Lay the pattern flat and cut the number of pieces needed. If patterned fabric is being used, cut one piece and use it for a pattern.

With the right sides together sew the lining to the bottom edge of the jabot (*sew the ruffle into the seam*) turn it right side out and press a knife edge.

Sew bottom seam

Insert ruffle

Press knife edge

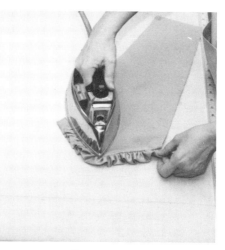

Press ruffle

54

If trim is being used, try gluing it on before sewing. To keep the stiches from showing, open the jabot and sew the trim through the seam allowance but not the lining, then finish the corner by hand *(or sew it all by hand)*.

Glue trim   Sew trim

Now, with the lining side out, sew all (4) of the edges together in a single seam. Turn the jabot right side out, center the seam, press it lightly *(do not press sharp creases at the folds)* and make a finished seam across the top.

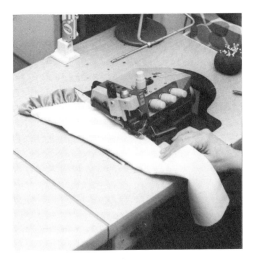

Sew seams   Turn right side out

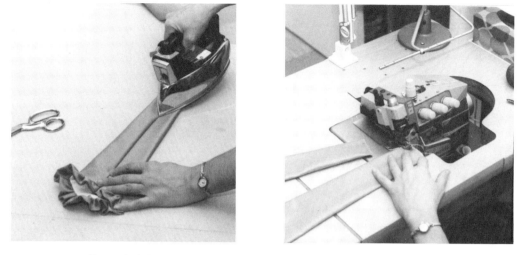

Press lightly   Finish tops

To make the reverse style, use the same patterns but leave the bottom of the face fabric straight. Seam the face fabric and facing separately, then lay the seam of the facing along the fold of the face fabric and cut the bottom, with the high point of the angle on the fold of the face fabric.

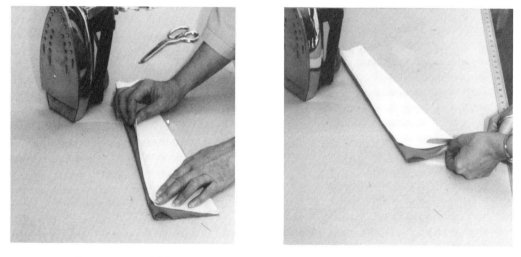

Lay seam on fold   Cut angle

Turn the facing right side out and pin it inside the jabot, matching the high and low points. Seam the bottom edges together, from the facing side and clip the corners. Turn the jabot right side out so that the facing fits smoothly inside. Press the bottom into a knife edge, align the seams, press it lightly and make a finished seam across the top.

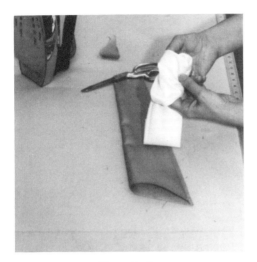

Turn facing

Insert facing

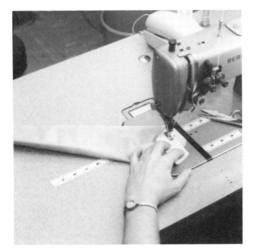

Sew bottom seam

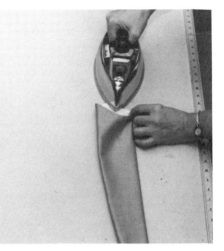

Press knife edge

There are two ways of making double, reverse style jabots. 1. Make one by the pattern and one (1″) narrower than the pattern and attach it on the top of the larger one. 2. Square a piece of paper (19″) wide and (5″) longer than the high point of the valance. Fold it in half lengthwise *(See diagram)*. Cut the lining (¼″) narrower at the top.

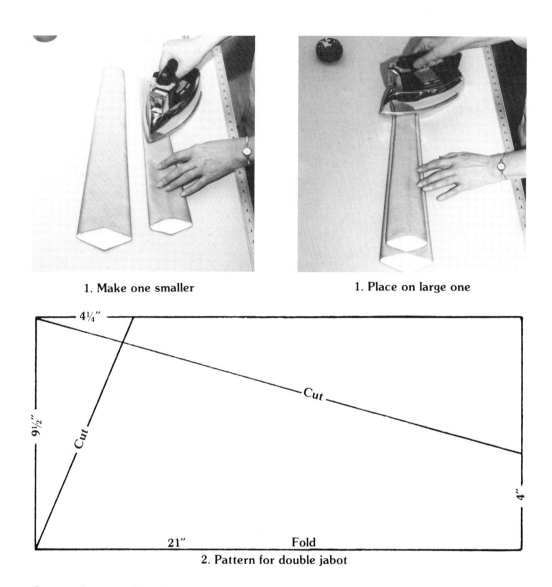

1. Make one smaller

1. Place on large one

4¼″

9½″

Cut

Cut

4″

21″   Fold

2. Pattern for double jabot

Cut and assemble the jabots in the same manner as the single reverse style. Fold it in half and draw a line so the back portion is (½″) wider than the front portion, then sew along the line. Carefully center the seam and flatten the jabot. Press it lightly and make a finished seam across the top.

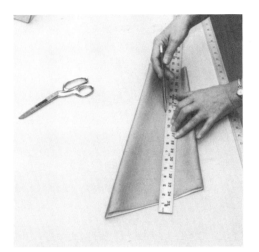

Mark stitching line

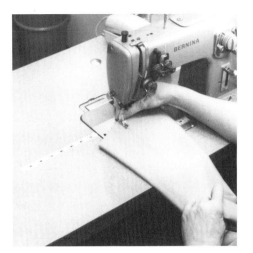

Sew division seam

Center jabot seam

Press lightly

The short cascade style jabot is the answer to using large Queen Anne or Original Style swags in a bay or corner windows.

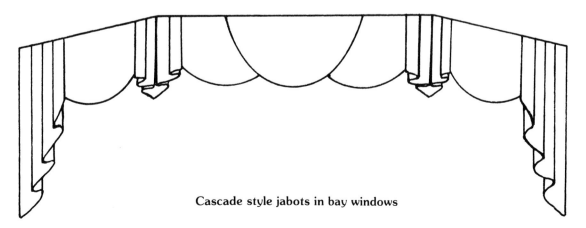

Cascade style jabots in bay windows

59

The jabot is made in much the same manner as the cascade, with the high point even with the swag where they meet. The length is a matter of preference, whether it is a little longer or the same length as the swag. *(Slight variations may occur when setting the high point exact.)*

The cut length of the jabot is (2″- 2½″) longer than the finished length. To determine the cut width, allow for (4 - 6) triple folds (2¾″ - 3¼″) a (1″) overlap on each side and (⅜″) seams. *(When used in combination with side cascades (See Section 10) folds should be the same size.)*

Example: 4 triple folds = 12 × 2¾″ = 33″ + 2 x 1″ overlaps + 2 x ⅜″ seams = 35¾″ cut width.

This style of jabot is either self or contrast lined and both pieces are cut the same size. When using patterned fabric, cut one and use it for a pattern. Pin the facing to the jabot and sew a (⅜″) seam. Press the seam toward the face. *(Gluing the trim in place makes it easier to sew.)* Open the jabot and sew the trim through the seam allowance, then finish the corners by hand. Make a finished seam across the top, mark the folds and pin them in place. Adjust the length to fit the swags and staple it onto the board.

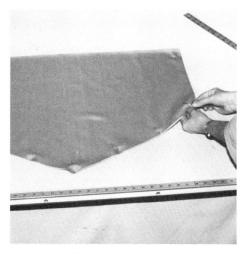
Pin edges together

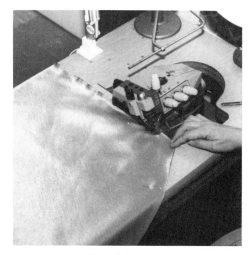
Sew ⅜″ seam

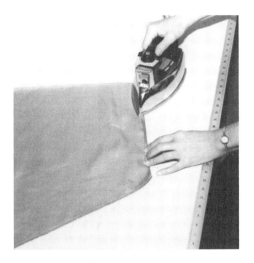

Press seams

Glue trim

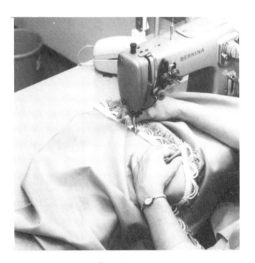

Sew trim

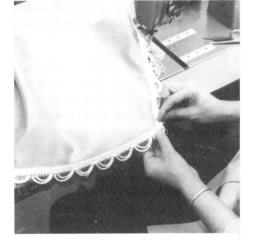

Hand stitch corners

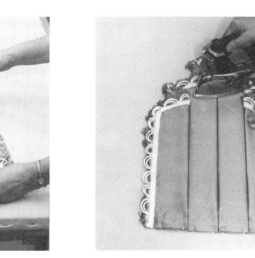

Fold toward center

Press lightly

SECTION 11

THE AUSTRIAN SWAG VALANCE

The Austrian swag really has two styles. One is made in the same manner as Austrian shades, with the rows of shirring making the decorative feature of the swag. The other one is made in the same way as the Empire swag *(See Section 9)* but is shirred rather than pleated into folds, with jabots covering the seams.

The Style I swag is used primarily for bedrooms and bathrooms, since it lends itself to soft delicate fabrics *(voiles, satins, crepes, etc.).* The Style II swag is usually made of fabrics other than sheers *(sateens, polished cottons, etc.)* with slightly larger swags.

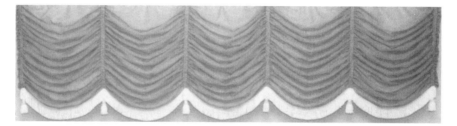

Style I swag. Single shirring

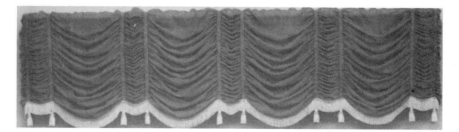

Style I swag. Variation of shirring

To calculate the yardage for Style I, determine the number of swags (10″ - 14″) that will fit across the face of the board (1″ x 8″) or (1″ x 6″) plus returns. Add (2″ - 2½″) for each swag (2″) for each return and (1½″) for each side hem. Allow (3) times the finished length for sheer and very light weight fabrics, and (2¾″) times the finished length for slightly heavier fabrics.

When made of very light weight fabrics, such as voile and batiste, this style is usually unlined. If lining is to be used, it can either be cut the same size and sewn with the face fabric, as if it were unlined or cut to the exact finished size, like a lambrequin *(See Section 7)* with the bottom scalloped, to fit the shirred face.

To make the unlined valance, cut the fabric to size *(seam if necessary)* and press a (1½″) single hem on each side. Fold and press a crease from top to bottom, to use as a guide, where each row of shirring tape will be sewn.

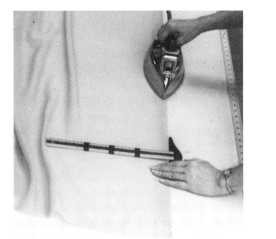

Press side hem

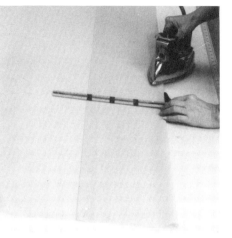

Measure return

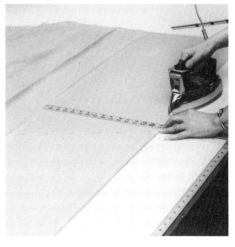

Press guide line

Now, using the crease as a guide, sew each row of shirring tape *(use double cord tape)* in place. Pull the cords out of the tape (¾″) from the top and bar-tack the cords in place to secure them at the bottom.

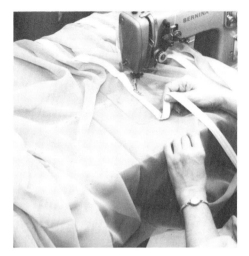

Sew tapes in place

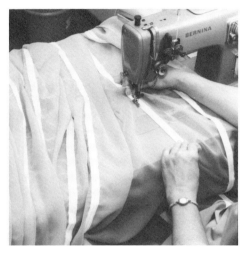

Sew other side

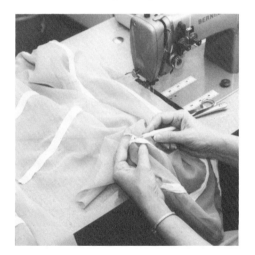

Pull cords free

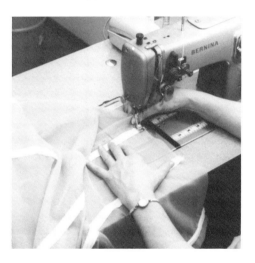

Bar-tack cords

Serge, make a finished seam or small hem at the top and sew a row of gathering stitches near the edge. Then, with the fabric wrong *(or lining)* side up, sew the fringe so that it just covers the raw edge. Turn it right side up and stitch near the top edge of the fringe. *(This encases the raw edge.)*

64

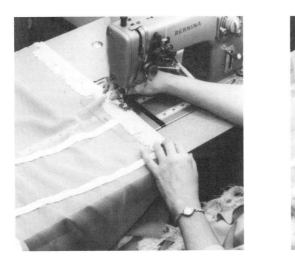

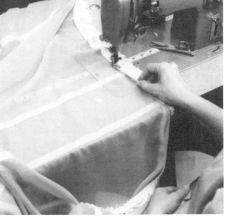

Sew fringe on wrong side   Sew fringe on right side

Pull the cords to the exact finished length, *(allow (2″) on the board)* and tie them together. Adjust the gathers and sew weighted tassels *(or heavy weights)* at the bottom of each tape.

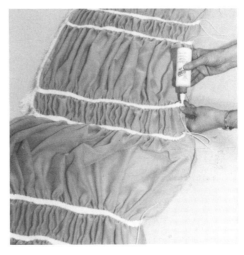

Pull cords   Glue tied cords

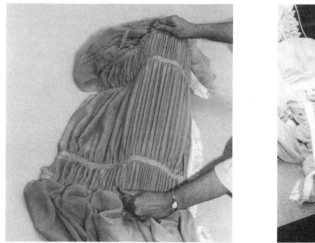

Adjust gathers

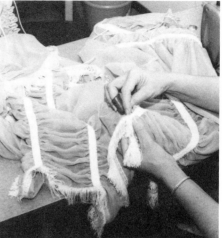

Sew weighted tassels

Prepare the board *(See Section 15)* and draw a line (2″) from the front. Mark the placement of each tape and staple the valance in place, at each cord, then ease the fullness between them by pulling the gathering stitches. Turn it upside down and mount the brackets and rods.

Mark board

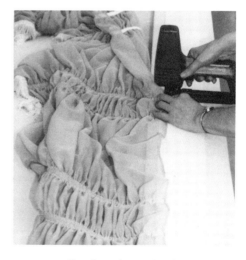

Staple valance in place

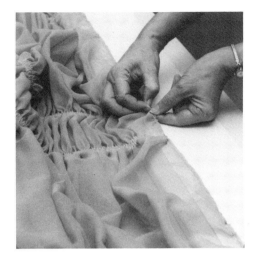

Ease fullness

If the valance is to be lined, with a separate lining, cut the lining about (8″) longer than the high point of the swag and wide enough to cover the front and ends of the board, plus side hems.

Make a scallop pattern the size *(width, depth and shape of the scallops)* that the shirred swag makes when it falls into place. Mark and cut the bottom edge of the lining into the number of scallops needed.

Make pattern of scallop

Scalloped lining

With the cords bar-tacked in place and the right sides together, carefully pin the face fabric to the scalloped lining. Sew a (⅜″) seam, clip the corners and turn it right side out. Press the seam into a knife edge and sew the trim through the seam. *(Try gluing the trim before sewing.)* Finish the top edge of the lining so it is (2″) longer than the finished length.

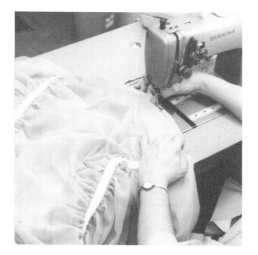
Sew bottom seam

Press a knife edge

Glue trim before sewing

Pull the cords to the exact finished length *(allow (2″) on the board)* and tie them together. Adjust the gathers and sew weighted tassels at the bottom of each tape *(or use end boards as shown for Style II)*. Mark the placement of the shirring tapes at the top of the lining and proceed in the same manner as for the unlined valance.

To make the Style II swag, follow the instructions for the Empire Swag *(See Section 9)* for calculating the yardage *(bias cut preferred)* cutting and assembling. Before finishing the top and bottom, insert a cord between the lining and face fabric at each seam. Sew shirring tape on the (1½") single side hems. Bar-tack through the cords about (¾") from the bottom.

Insert a cord

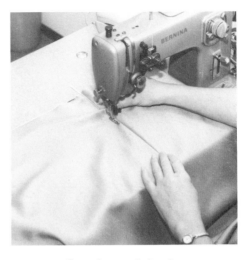
Sew the cords in place

Sew shirring tape

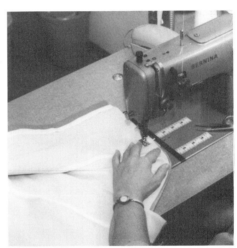
Bar-tack cords

Serge or make a finished seam across both the top and bottom of the valance. Sew the trim in the same manner as the unlined, Style I swag or make a small blind hem.

Free the cords, through the lining, near the top and pull them to the exact length *(allow (2") on the board)*. Tie a knot and adjust the gathers.

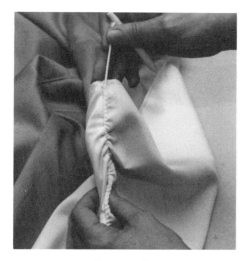

Free cords

Pull cords

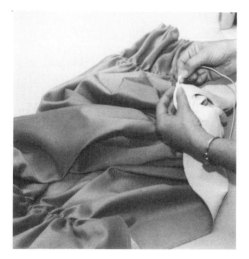

Tie a knot

Adjust gathers

Make the jabots *(See Section 10).*

Prepare the valance board and also two end boards *(See Section 15).* Draw a line (2″) from the front of the board, mark the position of each seam and staple the valance in place. Center a jabot over a seam, adjust it so that the high point is even with the high point of the valance and staple it in place. Then, staple the other jabots in place, the same distance from the front of the board.

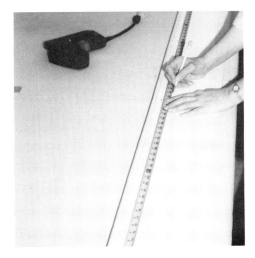

Mark board

Staple center

Staple valance in place

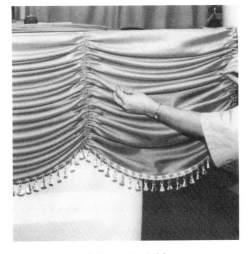

Adjust the folds

Adjust length of jabot

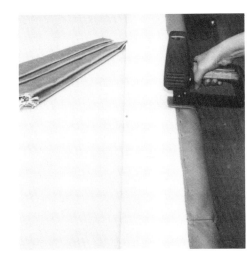

Staple jabots in place

Turn the board upside down and attach the end boards. This keeps the valance from pulling in at the sides *(See Section 9).*

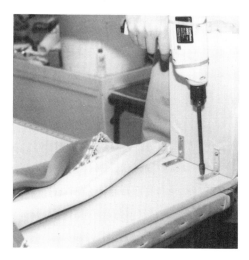

Attach the end boards

Mount the brackets and rods on the board ready for installation *(See Section 15).*

SECTION 12

THE QUEEN ANNE SWAG

This is the most well known of all swag treatments. The swags are beautiful with or without trim and can be assembled in various ways.

NOTE: Printed patterns are available for Sections 9, 12 & 14 (*Sections 10 & 13 are included*).

Queen Anne Style   Classic arrangement

Queen Anne style   Regency arrangement

Queen Anne style   Georgian arrangement

Since swag treatments are *(usually)* mounted at the ceiling, the instructions will be for the most popular size (38″- 40″) wide, (19″- 20″) drop.

To determine the number of swags needed, allow the full width of the swag for the first one and half the width for each additional one. The high point will be too high if they do not overlap half way. *(The size can be adjusted slightly without changing the pattern.)*

Each swag will take (1⅓) yards of both the face fabric and lining. *(Make allowance for pattern repeats.)* The cascades will take (2) yards each *(See Section 10).*

To make a pattern for seamless bias cut swags, square a piece of paper about (30″ x 45″). Draw a perpendicular line (7¼″) long, near one end of the paper. Measure (40½″) along the straight edge, then, measure up (28½″) and draw a line near the side to mark the bottom width. Next, draw an angled line (38¾″) long, from the top of the short line, to the line near the side. Finish the pattern by drawing a curved line across the bottom, then, cut it out.

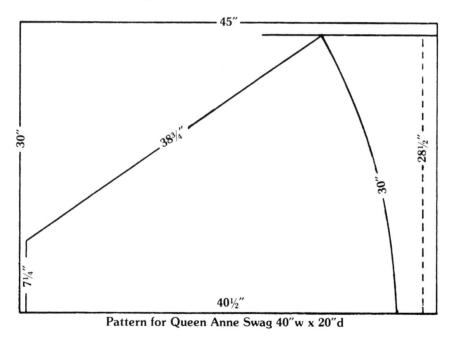

Pattern for Queen Anne Swag 40″w x 20″d

Lay the fabric on the table with the selvage against the table ruler and square the end. Fold the fabric diagonally so the squared end also fits along the table ruler.

74

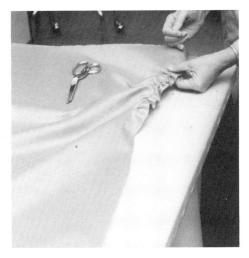

Pull thread   Square fabric

Lay the pattern with the longest side on the fold. Cut all of the swag and lining pieces in the same manner. *(Make the diagonal fold on the lining fabric the opposite direction.)* This assures all pieces being cut the same direction *(top of swags)* of the fabric and on a true bias. When using patterned fabric, cut one piece and use it for a pattern. *(See Section 13 for the cascades.)*

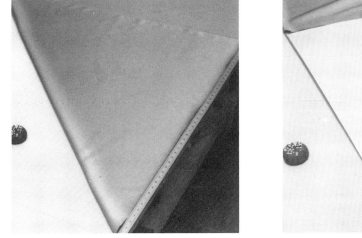

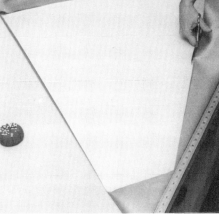

Fold diagonally   Pattern layout

Fit the swag and lining, face sides, together and pin the bottom edges. Serge or sew a (³/₈″) seam and press it toward the face fabric. Then, with the swag laying open, machine sew the trim *(through the seam but not the lining).* This gives stability to the bias cut and keeps it from stretching. If trim is not being used press a hem around the seam.

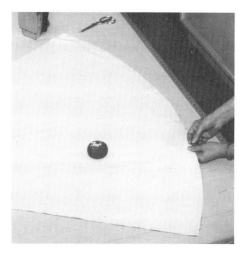

Pin bottom edges

Sew bottom seam

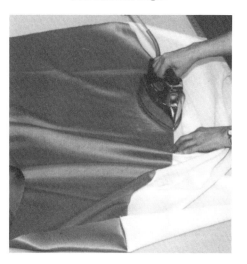

Press seam

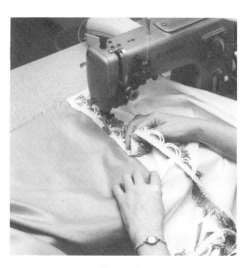

Sew trim

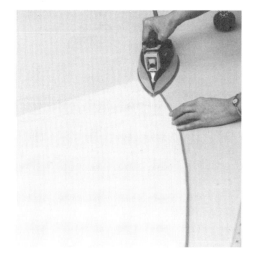

Press hem

With the swags right side out, smooth the swag and pin the edges together. *(The lining will be larger on hemmed swags and will need to be trimmed.)* Serge or make a finished seam around the edges, to keep it from fraying.

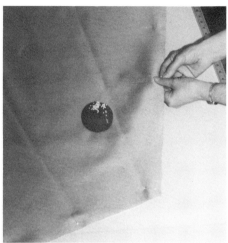

Pin edges together

Pin hemmed swag

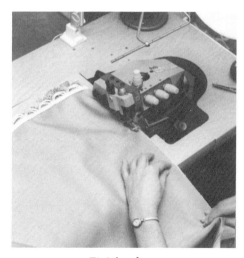

Finish edges

To mark the folds, start (½") from the top of the pattern, and mark at (5¼") intervals. Make another row of marks at (5¼") intervals (1¼") from the edge and (1¾") below each of the previous marks. *(Adjustments can be made here for different size swags. Experiment.)* Draw a zig-zag line from one mark to the next, ending near the bottom outside edge of the pattern.

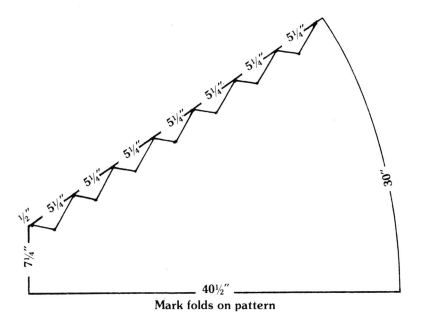

Mark folds on pattern

Cut the pattern along the zig-zag line and trace the pattern *(cut out)* on both sides of each swag (¼″) from the edge. *(Stitch along the zig-zag line to assure perfect folding again after cleaning the swags.)* Then, make a mark on the long sections of the zig-zag line (1⅝″) from the inside point.

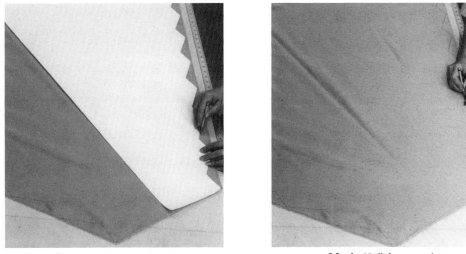

Trace pattern cut out   Mark 1⅝″ from point

Fold the swag by bringing the first inside point of the zig-zag line to (¼″) from the top edge with the lines matched on both sides of the fold. Make each additional fold by bringing the inside point to the line (1⅝″) from the previous fold and pin it securely, so that the line across the top is perfectly straight. *(Adjust the two center folds on each side slightly if necessary.)* For ease in handling, sew the folded swag, along the line, with long loose stitches *(that can be pulled out, easily, for cleaning the swag flat).*

78

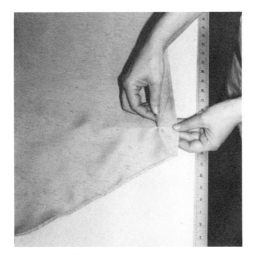

Pin through 1st fold

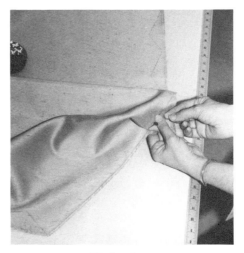

Pin in place

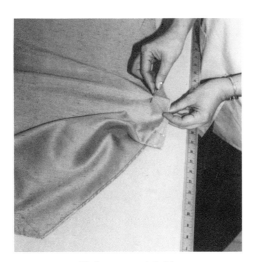

Pick up next fold

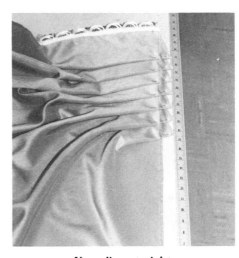

Keep line straight

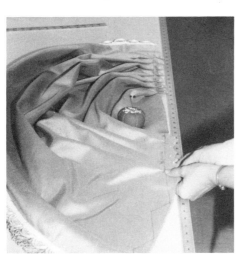

Fold other side

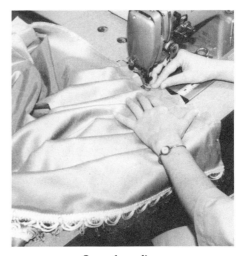

Sew along line

79

Folded swag

Prepare the board *(See Section 15)*. If this style is not mounted at the ceiling, do not use the polyfoam.

Measure the exact width of the swag and mark the placement of each one on the board. Staple the swags in place, then, adjust the cascades so the high point of the cascade is even with or slightly lower *(never higher)* than the swag where they meet and staple them in place.

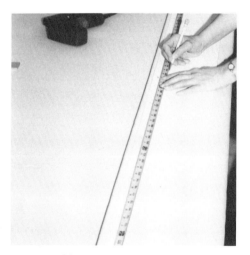

Mark swag placement

Staple swags in place

80

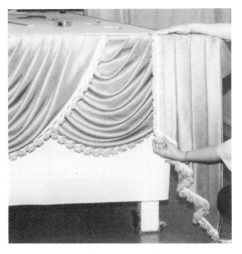

Adjust cascades

The swag treatment looks very different with the cascades mounted under the swags.

Queen Anne style   Classic arrangement

Turn the completed board upside down and mount the brackets and rods, ready for installation *(See Section 15).*

SECTION 13

CASCADES

Cascades are the cascading end pieces that are used with both Queen Anne and Original Style swags.

The high point of the cascade should be even with the swag at the point where they meet. The length is usually a little less than half the length of the draperies *(some people like them a little shorter)*, but are attractive longer or even floor length, when used over sheers without overdrapes.

A pattern is not necessary, since it is all straight lines. Each cascade takes approximately (2) yards, plus allowance for pattern repeats. They are usually self lined so the pattern will be upside down in the lining *(facing)*. When using velveteen, allow ($2\frac{3}{4}$) yards for each cascade.

The width and number of folds is variable, but, should cover between ($\frac{1}{4}$) and ($\frac{1}{3}$) of a single swag. *(The high point between the swag and cascade should be even with the high points between the cascades.)* There is usually four ($2\frac{3}{4}$″ - $3\frac{1}{4}$″) folds in a cascade, but on very narrow windows three folds look better.

To determine the cut width, allow for (4) or (3) triple folds, a (1″) overlap on the short side, the return ($5\frac{1}{2}$″) or ($7\frac{1}{4}$″) and ($\frac{3}{8}$″) seams.

Example: 4 triple folds = 12 × $2\frac{3}{4}$″ = 33″ + 1″ overlap + $7\frac{1}{4}$″ return + 2 × $\frac{3}{8}$″ seams = 42″ cut width.

Special care must be given to printed or woven patterns. The cascades are folded in opposite directions *(mirror images)* so a different part of the pattern will be showing, unless, it is either a symmetrical or a reverse drop pattern *(See Book I Section 10)*. Other patterns can be cut so at least the same part *(coloring)* of the pattern shows.

Square and cut two pieces of fabric (67″) long *(or any desired length)*. Lay them *(in the same direction)* face side together, with the selvages against the table ruler *(See Book I Section 8)*. Trim the width to (42″).

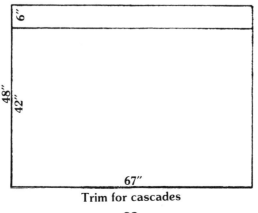

Trim for cascades

82

Draw a line from a point (19″) from the end on one side to a point (19″) from the opposite end on the other side. Cut along the line and pin the edges together. If the fabric has a one direction sheen or pattern, use the two pieces from one end *(the direction the draperies were made)* for the face and the other two pieces for the lining *(facing)*.

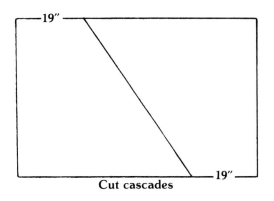

Cut cascades

Seam the sides and bottom, turn it right side out and press the seams toward the face fabric. Then with the cascade spread open, sew the trim *(through the seam but not the facing)* along the short and diagonal edges of the cascade. Hand stitch the trim at the corner and bottom. Press the long side into a knife edge and if trim is not being used, press the other seams into a knive edge also.

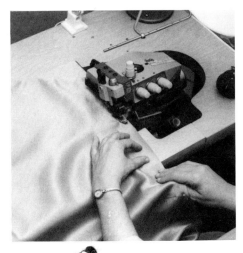

Sew ⅜″ seams

Press seams

83

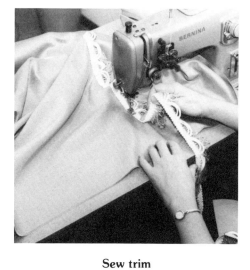

Sew trim

Hand stitch corners

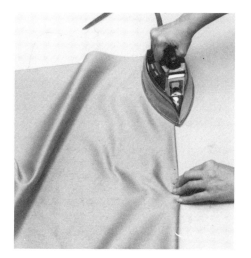

Press knife edge

Press the cascade so it is perfectly smooth, pin the top edges together and either serge it or make a finished seam. Mark the folds, near the top edge, pin them in place and press them lightly.

Pin top edges

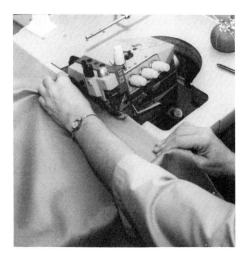

Make finished seam

Pin securely

Keep folds straight

Fold return back

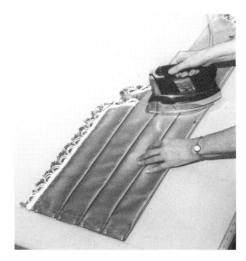

Press lightly

After the swags are in place, adjust the length of the cascade so the high point is even with *(or slightly lower than)* the swag where they meet and staple or tack them in place. The returns will be tacked at an angle to accommodate the thickness at the front of the board *(See Section 14 and 15)*.

Turn the board upside down and mount the brackets and rods while you have it on the table *(See Section 15)*.

SECTION 14

DEE'S ORIGINAL DESIGN SWAG

This has been the most popular of all the top treatments in our shops. Except for the straight lambrequin, it is the easiest to make *(and the most elegant)* of all the top treatments. It should be mounted at the ceiling, with the high point just below the top of the glass.

Original Design Regency arrangement

Original Design Georgian arrangement

Original Design Classic arrangement

87

The swag treatment looks very different with the cascades mounted under the swags. Any arrangement can be made with the small swags or with (54") fabric. By reversing the angle of the bias for half of the swags, nearly every arrangement can be made with the large size, using (48") fabric.

NOTE: Printed patterns are available for Sections 9, 12 & 14 *(Sections 10 & 13 are included).*

The figures used here are for the most frequently used sizes using (48") plain fabric. The swags can be made from (36"- 45") wide with a drop of (18"- 21"). Only the smallest ones *(up to 36" x 18"- 19")* can be made from (48") fabric without an exposed seam. Avoid styles where the seams cannot be hidden. *(Some printed patterns can be perfectly matched and the seams would be undiscernable, but, brocades and plain fabrics should never have an exposed seam.)*

To determine the number of swags needed, decide how they are to be assembled and the preferred size. The first one takes the full width and each additional one takes half the width.

When making this style of swag treatment, the cascades will be cut along with the swags. Each swag takes (1½) yards, plus (½) yard extra for the first bias cut and each cascade takes approximately (2) yards. *(See Section 13.)* Make allowances for pattern matching, so the swags will be identical. The pattern in the lining *(facing)* will be upside down. *(Napped fabric should not be made upside down.)*

Place the fabric, face side up, against the table ruler and square the end. Allow (19") for the short side of the cascade, on one side of the fabric and (19") plus the width of the fabric *(or table)* on the other side. Using a long straight edge *(or ruler)* mark the diagonal line and cut the fabric into the number of (54") pieces required. *(Cut patterned fabrics on the repeats.)* Then, measure (19") on the short side of the remaining fabric and square it off. This will make the lining *(facing)* of the other cascade.

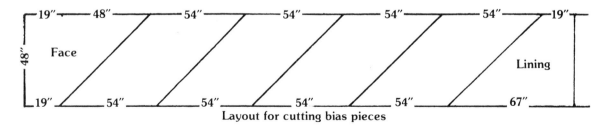
Layout for cutting bias pieces

To cut the other cascade pieces, square a piece of fabric (67") long and trim it to the exact width needed for the cascades *(See Section 13)*. Lay it face side up against the table ruler. Trim the angled pieces, on the long side, to the exact width and lay them face side down on it. Pin the straight sides in place and draw a line diagonally from the short side of one piece to the short side of the other piece. Cut along the line and pin the angled sides together. *(Follow the directions in Section 13.)*

88

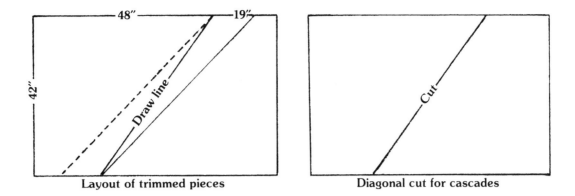

Layout of trimmed pieces   Diagonal cut for cascades

The yardage for the swag lining is (1½) yards for each swag, plus (1½) yards extra for the first bias cut.

Lay the lining fabric, face side down against the table ruler. Mark the first diagonal cut starting from the end of the fabric and proceed in the same manner as for the face fabric. If the lining is rolled so the face side is up on the table, *reverse the angle of the cuts.*

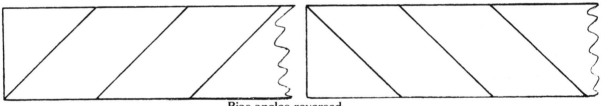

Bias angles reversed

To sew the seams for the swags, bring the acute angle of the selvage to the obtuse angle of the same selvage, then sew and trim the selvage from the cut edges to the fold. Sew both sides of all the pieces *(face fabric and lining)* in the same mammer.

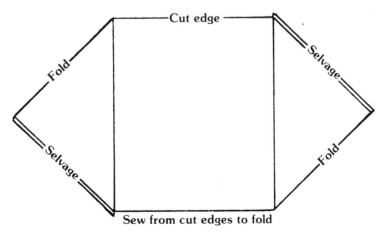

Sew from cut edges to fold

Lay the seamed, folded pieces on the table with the cut edges toward you. *(The seams will be on opposite sides in the lining.)* Cut along the folds at the

89

sides. For oversized *(or very small)* swags make the cut between the seam and the fold.

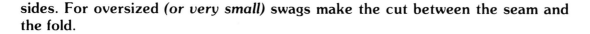

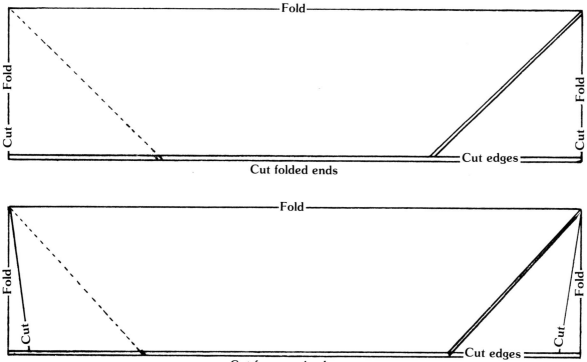

Lay it out flat and press the seams, one way in the face fabric and the opposite way in the lining.

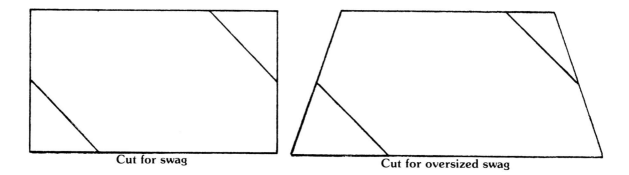

To determine the cut width of the bottom of the swag, loop a string from the side of the table at the desired width and depth, allowing (2″) for mounting, then measure the string. The cut width at the top should be about (2″) wider than the finished width.

To shape the swag, lay the face fabric on the table, face side up, with the lining on top of it, face side down and the bottom edges against the ruler. Align the top seams and top edges.

The center area of the swag is (13″) less than the finished width. Starting at the top seam (½″) from the top edge, mark the center area (also the exact center top and bottom) and make a mark (7½″) out on each side. Measure the bottom width and draw a line from the outside mark at the top, to the bottom. Then, make a curved line at the bottom, from the center to (4½″) from the bottom at the sides.

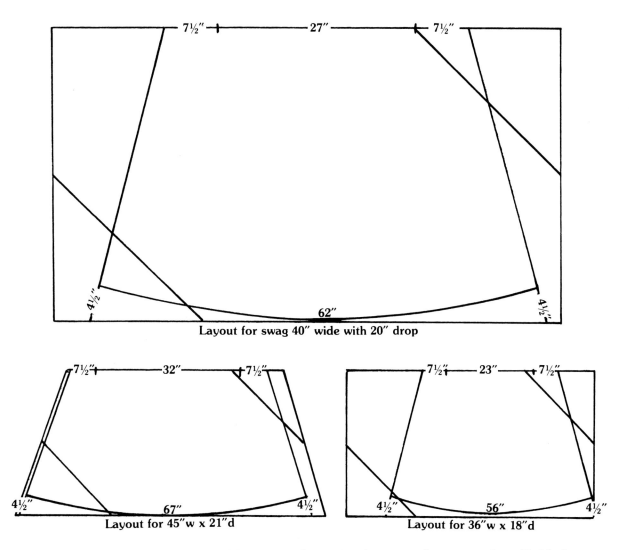

Layout for swag 40″ wide with 20″ drop

Layout for 45″w x 21″d

Layout for 36″w x 18″d

Cut the side and curved bottom, then pin the cut edges together. Fold the swag in the center and cut the rest of the bottom and the other side. Pin the cut edges together, the rest of the way around it. Then, using it for a pattern, align the seams and cut the other swags. (Pin only the bottom edges of the other swags.)

Make curved line

Pin cut side and bottom

Cut balance of swag

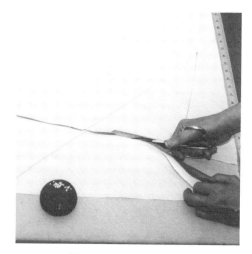

Use swag for pattern

Sew the bottom using a (⅜″) seam. Then, if trim is being used, press the seam toward the face fabric. With the swag opened, sew the trim through the seam allowance *(this gives more stability)*. If trim is not being used, press a small hem around the seam.

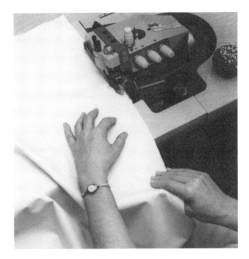

Sew bottom seam

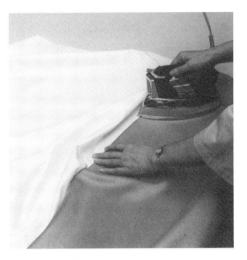

Press toward face

Sew trim

Press hem

Lay the swag face side up, smooth it and pin the cut edges together. *(The lining will be larger if the swag is hemmed.)* Serge around the edges or make a finished seam and trim the edges.

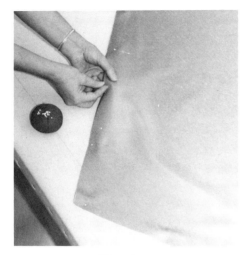

Pin edges

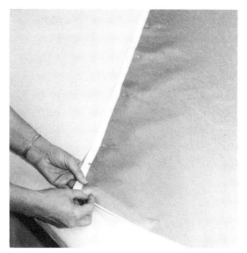

Pin hemmed swag

Finish edges

The swag is now ready to fold. Press it and mark the center first, then mark the center area. Angle the ruler from the mark at the top to approximately (2½″) from the side at the bottom, on each side and divide the distance into (7) equal spaces. Mark with pins first if you're not sure of the size. It's easy to adjust, simply by changing the side angles.

Mark center

Mark center area

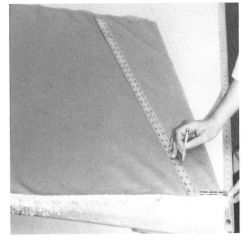

Mark folds

Start at the bottom, pin through the first mark *(about ⅛" deep)* making a fold to the next mark. Make each fold in turn, ending at the top by putting the pin straight through the mark. Fold the other side in the same manner. Pin it to the edge of the table and adjust the folds. Then fold all of the swags in the same manner.

Pin through fold marks

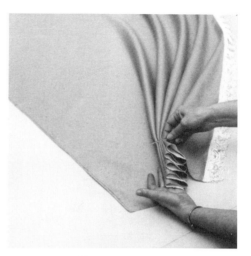

Keep folds even

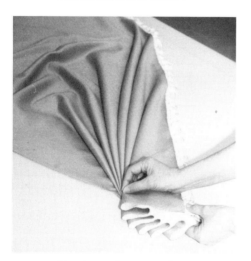

Pin through top mark

Fold other side

Pin swag to table

Adjust folds

Folded swag

Prepare the board *(See Section 15)* with a strip of (½″) polyfoam around the front edge of it. This keeps it flat against the ceiling. Mark the swag placement on the board so that the seam in the swag will be covered with the next swag. *(Small swags can be arranged in any manner.)*

Mark swag placement

Tack the first swag on the board, replacing the pins with (¾″) nails. Adjust the folds and staple the swag in place. Continue in this manner until all of the swags are in place. Then, adjust the length of the cascades so the high point is even with the swag, where they meet and staple or nail them in place. The return will be tacked at an angle to accommodate the thickness at the front of the board *(or to fit a slanted ceiling).*

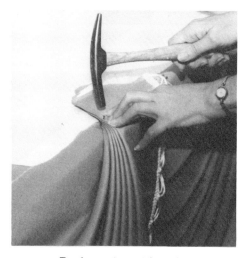

Replace pins with nails

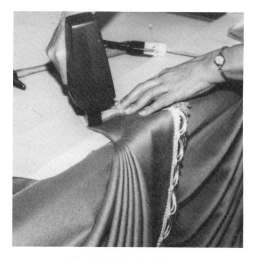

Staple folds in place

Adjust cascades

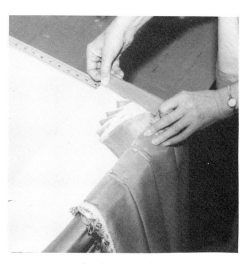

Angle cascade

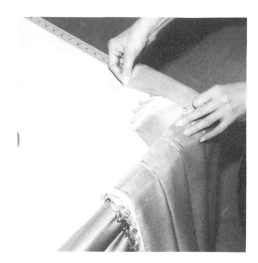

Angle for slant ceiling

Turn the board upside down and mount the brackets and rods while you have it on the table *(See Section 15)*.

SECTION 15

INSTALLING

The ease of installing comes with doing first things first. Preparation should be made for installation while the top treatments *(and draperies)* are being made.

The rods for pleated or shirred valances should project (6″) or (8″- 9″) from the wall for single and double draperies respectively.

The brackets, for shirred *(rod pocket)* valances, must be placed **exact** distances apart *(See Section 3)* so the gathers can be evenly distributed the full length of the rod.

All other valances are attached to boards. A (1″x 6″) measures (5½″) and a (1″x 8″) measures (7¼″). Use them for single and double draperies respectively. *(Redwood is light weight and warps very little.)* If a valance board is to be mounted against a slanted ceiling *(or if more projection is needed)* attach a (1″x 1″) to the back of the board.

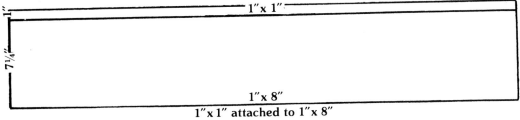

1″x 1″ attached to 1″x 8″

To prepare a valance board, cut it the exact length needed *(make allowances for inside measurement)*. Whenever a valance is mounted at the ceiling *(most of them are)*, staple a strip of (½″) polyfoam along the top, front edge of the board to hold it tight against the ceiling. The straight hanging lambrequin and sometimes the box pleated valance are the only styles I recommend mounting with velcro. Staple the hook part of the velcro to the face edges of the board.

Cover board

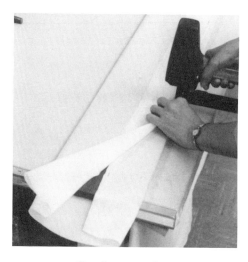

Staple near edge

Staple foam strip

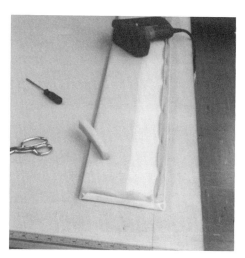

Foam strip in place

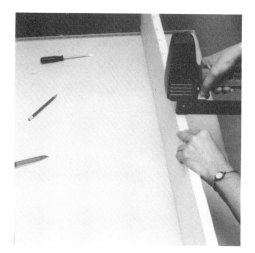

Staple velcro

Determine the number and size of the angle brackets needed, by the width of the board and the weight they'll be holding up.

While the valance board *(or cornice)* is still on the table, after completion, turn it upside down and mount the brackets. Then, place washers under the ceiling clips and rod ends to keep the rod (rods) level over the brackets. Place screw eyes near the back of the board to accommodate the returns, when using single rods.

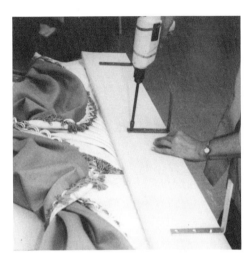

Mount brackets

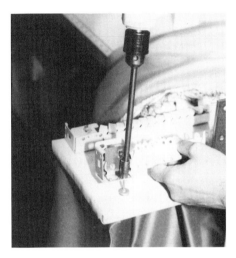

Washers under rod ends

Mounted rods

If the board is to be mounted against a slanted ceiling, straighten the brackets to the angle needed. *(Put the bracket in a vise and tighten it until the exact degree of the angle is achieved.)*

101

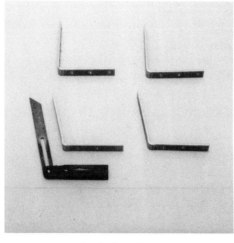

Angle brackets

Now, with the brackets and the rods in place, it is rather simple to prop the valance board tight against the ceiling *(or at any given height)* with (1"x 4"s) covered and padded on the ends, while securing it with long screws into the plate. If this cannot be done, mark the screw holes and let the board down. Use wing dings, molly or toggle bolts, then put the board back into position and secure it.

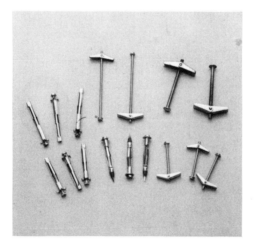

Wing dings, molly and toggle bolts

Use the same technique to install cornices. Prop the cornice in place and mark the bracket placement on the wall. Let the cornice down, remove the brackets and mount them on the wall, then push *(or place)* the cornice into place and secure the brackets back on the board.

Mount the cord pulleys on the wall and hang the draperies.

Adjust the folds in the valances *(and draperies)* and the job is complete.

Notes

Notes

Notes

Notes

Notes

Notes